Great Care,
Every Patient

Great Care, Every Patient

A Physician's Guide to Improving Any Process

David J Norris, MD, MBA

Paperback: 978-1-64746-300-7
Hardback: 978-1-64746-301-4
Ebook: 978-1-64746-302-1
Library of Congress Control Number: 2020909740

Dedication

To my wife, Megan, and children, Jacob and Adelle, who have supported me every day. Thank you for your patience. To Chad, thank you for your insight and experience in process improvement that helped me understand the nuances of service operations.

Contents

Preface

Many years ago, I was honored to be given leadership positions within my hospital and group and was asked to fix a hospital-based clinic. I wasn't given any directions other than "fix it." Many lessons were learned from mistakes and successes during that process. Those lessons are succinctly shared with you, the reader, in this book.

Most physicians do not have the time or energy to return to school and earn an MBA. This book is my attempt to provide my fellow physicians and healthcare providers with knowledge and insight to create a service that serves their patients well without going to business school.

Yours in service,
David

1

Introduction

Thanks and Congrats

Thank you for picking up this book. I consider it a great honor that you would invest in yourself and utilize this book to improve your business. After you complete your journey through the material, you will be able to improve any process and design a service that delights your patients.

The material discussed within is something physicians and other healthcare leaders desperately need. It is information that doctors, or other healthcare professionals, are not taught in most professional schools or graduate medical training programs.

Before you get too far in, let me say that this isn't some high-fluting theory book on process improvement. I'm sharing with you what I've found to work best in my process improvement projects. I've also seen these tools work well in the hands of my clients. I won't make it complicated. I believe in doing just the opposite. Make it as simple as possible. There won't be any fluff or fancy talk here, and you won't learn stuff that you won't use. Unlike biochemistry in medical school, the tools I'll teach you will be useful. You won't waste your time with this book. How often have you used the Kreb's cycle in your practice? I guarantee you will use the information contained within these pages regularly.

I would also like to congratulate you, as you've taken a significant step in the right direction. What you are about to learn will make yourself a better leader, a better business owner, and a better physician. I think you will be astounded by the impact implementing these practices can have on your bottom line. By the end of this book, you will be able to understand how to:

➢ Evaluate any process for effectiveness.
➢ Determine the points of inefficiency and ineffectiveness present in the process.
➢ Understand the necessary steps required to improve the process.
➢ Be well-equipped to tackle any process improvement problem you may face, no matter the environment, organization, or situation.

Why I Created This Book

I've assisted many organizations with change implementation. What I will teach you has worked in my practice, my hospital, other physicians' clinics, on the floor of manufacturing companies, and at service-based organizations outside of healthcare. I want you to become the most effective change leader in your organization. If you implement the tools within this book, you will be taking a step in the right direction towards that goal.

A lot of this knowledge I've learned from my colleague, Chad Raney. When we started working on this project, he brought different perspectives and experiences. Chad isn't a physician. He trains pilots at a flight simulator center. They are a service industry, much like those in healthcare, and there are a lot of parallels to the issues he faces, just like any service industry or service organization would face. Chad also brought his experiences as a patient. He saw firsthand the effects a poor process has on a patient. He switched physicians more than once because the operational processes in the physicians' offices were designed so poorly and made the customer experience dissatisfying. Chad, unlike many patients, has the knowledge to make things better. He also has a friend who is a physician that also wants to help his fellow physicians.

My mission and purpose throughout this book are to help healthcare professionals obtain the practice they desire by improving their business intelligence. There are four critical pieces you will need to develop: people, processes, performance, and profits. In my first book, I taught you how to read and use financial statements so you can make better business decisions. In this book, we will examine the processes and the performance of your practice. Being able to improve the operations of your clinic will dramatically improve your bottom line and help you create the practice you desire.

Processes Will Either Make or Cost You Money

Process improvement is just like other things in life. If you cannot understand something, you cannot control it. That lack of understanding will impede your ability to make significant gains towards efficiency and effectiveness. It's similar to medical school. You will have a hard time understanding pharmacology if you don't understand physiology. Disease states and how to treat them become much easier if you know the basics. Process improvements are the same. We will have a hard time making our patient care better if we don't understand the fundamentals of the processes and how to improve them.

> ➢ **Effective and efficient processes are critical.** We all want to deliver the right care to the right patient at the right time. It's easier said than done sometimes. How we provide that care will impact the patients' perception of the care we provide. Our systems must be efficient and as cost-effective as possible. They must also be as effective as possible.

> ➢ **Inefficient processes cost time and money.** If we have processes that require the work to be done a second time or delay diagnosis or treatment, those poor systems will cost us money, time, and our patients their health. We should strive to eliminate all possible inefficiencies and not waste our time and dollars and that of the patient as well.

➤ **Poor processes lead to low-quality outcomes.** Sloppy work leads to mediocre results. Despite this being a given, we must work to eliminate those processes that lead to poor outcomes. Poorly coordinated processes can lead a patient to discount our instructions, resulting in them being less likely to adhere to our therapy. Poor quality processes and their resultant outcomes hurt not only the patient but our practice as well.

➤ **Proper processes are efficient and improve quality.** Quality care is our goal. As budgets become tighter and regulations rise, efficient and effective processes are our best method of maintaining profitability so we may continue to care for our patients. We can design systems that provide excellent care and delight the patient.

➤ **Processes should be at the demand of the customer.** If you are doing something that the customer is not willing to pay for, does not add value, or is not a regulatory requirement, then you should ask, "Should we be doing that step or process?" If the answer is no, then consider eliminating it, as it is potentially a waste of time, energy, money, and resources.

What's the Problem?

Just like in medicine, we must first define the problem. Process implement expert Robert Humphrey said, "An undefined problem has an infinite number of solutions." Defining the problem is the crucial first step.

After working with many clinics and practices, the most common issue facing physicians is they don't have a good understanding of process improvement. They seem overwhelmed and don't know where to start. I believe that is because they haven't defined the problem. Therefore, just about any action or idea will sound good; everything seems like it'll work. But one bit of wisdom I can share with you is this: don't rush to apply a fix. Stop and spend some time thinking about the problem.

Spend some time thinking about the problem once it's clear what the problem is. Albert Einstein said, "If I had an hour to solve a problem, I spent 55 minutes thinking about the problem and five minutes thinking about the solutions." That is the key to the first step in process improvement. Take the necessary time to identify the real problems. Don't be quick to just slap a Band-Aid on the situation.

Imagine if a patient comes to us and says, "My belly hurts," and you say, "Oh, yeah, it's probably just the flu," and you send them out the door. You haven't identified the real problem. You need to identify the source of the problem. Is it appendicitis, a small bowel obstruction, ovarian cysts, a urinary tract infection, a kidney stone? It could be any number of things. We are trained to discover the real problem impacting our patient's health. We only need to apply those same principles to our practice. We should aim to figure out what the problems are that are keeping us from our goal of exemplary patient care. Once we've identified the issues, we can then focus on the solutions.

Just like a differential diagnosis, spend more time trying to figure out the problems that are keeping us from our goals and objectives. Only then can we solve the real problems, the root causes. However, to change things in your practice, you must be an effective leader. Without strong leadership, all the good plans you design will fail to reach maximum potential.

Qualities of Effective Change Leaders

I want you to be an effective change leader, no matter where you are. It's easy to spot an effective one. In my study on the art of leadership, I've discovered that great leaders have several things in common. The following are six specific characteristics.

The first quality is effective decision-making. Great leaders not afraid to make a decision. They realize that their decision is the best one they could make with the given information. Sometimes new information comes along and shows the first decision probably wasn't the best. Effective decision-making means that you're not afraid to make a decision, and you're also not married to the decision you make. That doesn't mean you waffle, but that you are more than willing and able to accept new data if it shows that the decision you made might've not been the best one. Effective decision-making keeps an open mind to new data.

The second characteristic is that they are mission- and purpose-driven. Effective leaders understand what it is they're doing and why they're doing it. That is the definition of your mission and purpose—what it is you do, and why you are doing it for the benefit of the patient. Sometimes we get a little lost in the weeds. We lose sight of why it is we do what we do, but effective change leaders understand that all decisions must be based upon the mission and purpose.

Thirdly, they know how to set valid activity and behavioral goals and objectives. They plan and understand what it is going to take for them to achieve that mission and purpose. These are defined as their objectives. Once they know their objectives, they set valid goals that support attaining those objectives. These goals are physical behaviors that lead them to their objectives. Let's assume I had the objective of losing ten pounds. Now I must establish valid goals, those physical activities that are valid and support my weight loss objective. These would be eating healthy foods, exercising every day, and getting the proper amount of rest. Those are valid goals that support those objectives. Drinking alcohol regularly, smoking, and eating cheesecake every day probably wouldn't support the objective of losing weight. Effective leaders know how to determine their objectives and set valid goals.

Sometimes when we're trying to change, we lose sight of what our goals and objectives are. Often we can find ourselves wasting time and energy doing tasks that don't directly support our objectives. "Does this goal support this objective?" is a question we should ask regularly. We're going to get into that later on in the course when we talk about benchmarking, process improvement, and quality improvement.

The fourth quality of effective leaders is their ability to identify and solve real problems. They are focused on solving real issues, not just stated or assumed problems. Adopting this characteristic will keep you from using Band-Aids to fix your problems. Instead, you will be able to create effective change. We're going to walk through a system that's going to get you there in this book.

The fifth characteristic is their ability to stay focused. Leaders remain focused on their mission and purpose. They stay focused on their objectives and goals and do so for a long time. Sometimes change stretches on for weeks, months, even years. Change will require a lot of hard work, and we can become easily distracted when we work and work and work, and do not see the immediate change we want. We must understand and acknowledge that change doesn't occur overnight. Remember, you didn't get to where you are today overnight, just as you didn't become a physician overnight. Change is a slow and gradual process. You arrived where you are today by a series of decisions in the past. Effective change leaders know how to stay focused because they are driven by mission and purpose. Perhaps the most valuable aspect of a growth mindset is realizing you don't have all the answers. You have developed the ability to ask questions and listen to the voice of the customer. You're able to determine their perspective, leanings, and pain points. The solutions you develop during a process change must address the concerns of the patient.

Finally, effective change leaders possess a growth mindset, which holds that things have the potential to improve. There are new ideas out there that might be useful in making things better. This is perhaps the most important quality for leading change. In an upcoming chapter, we're going to dive a little deeper into what it means to have a growth mindset because I think it's fundamental for you to have one when you're trying to lead effective change.

Being an effective change leader requires more than the six leadership characteristics listed above. As physicians, we have learned to manage these areas for ourselves. Decisive, well-informed decisions under pressure are routine in a day's work. Our experience is extremely valid to draw from; however, it is also our most deceiving weakness as business leaders responsible for a service organization. To truly be impactful in improving your processes, the following also needs to occur:

> ➢ Success is possible only if your employees understand, believe, and execute the business with the same vision you have for your practice.

> ➢ Employees must be able to have the flexibility to accommodate patients within certain parameters to "exceed the patient's expectations." Give them the power to solve their problems.

> ➢ Your job is to support, communicate, train, and coach your team until they are better at taking care of patients than you.

Your success as a physician is based on your performance, that of your team, and those processes you use in your practice. Your success as a business person is based on your team being able to execute your vision successfully. This reality is what creates the underlying need to shift where you choose to focus your efforts.

2

Mindset

In the previous chapter, I introduced the concept of a growth mindset. In working with leaders, I've discovered that their mindset is perhaps their most significant asset or liability. In this chapter, we will discuss mindset and how our mindset will affect, if not dictate, our success.

Meet Bill

Let's take a look at a physician I knew named Bill. He had been in practice for a number of years but was frustrated and came to me asking for help. He didn't understand what was going on in his practice. His patients were complaining. He and his staff were working as fast as they could. He was an excellent physician too. But why were they complaining? Was it something he was doing wrong? Was it the staff? Were patients expecting too much? He didn't have an idea, but he realized if he didn't do something soon, he would need to begin thinking about selling his practice and working for a local hospital. He was not there yet. Bill thought he knew the solution to the problem, but it never worked as he expected. He was getting frustrated and burned out.

In talking with Bill, he seemed to think he had all the answers. What he didn't realize, or accept, was there were times when he didn't. Bill was similar to a lot of physicians I worked with. When I first started working with them, they seemed to think they knew what was going on and had all the answers. If that was the case, why did they ask me for help? Because they eventually realized they didn't have all the answers. They were bringing with them a few biases. These biases, which sprout from a fixed mindset, compounded the problem. If Bill wanted to be an effective change leader, he needed to change his mindset. And that's what we did.

A while back, I conducted workshops with a mentor of mine. One of the topics I would teach was the topic of mindset. As I was preparing for my first lesson, I looked up the word *mindset* in the dictionary. It was defined as "*a person's established set of attitudes.*" When I first read that definition, I thought, *That makes sense. I understand what an attitude is.* I can identify bad attitudes pretty quickly in employees, patients, coworkers, and my children. But then I was curious about the definition of *attitude.* I discovered it is "*the way we think or feel.*" Once we understand how we think and feel, we can begin to have more control over how we lead.

So, if we hate process improvement and don't want to spend a lot of time on it, we are going to have actions and behaviors that lead us to avoid improving any process. We might think the change will be hard, or, even worse, we might think we have all the answers because we went to medical school and are smart. It's quite simple; those thoughts and feelings will lead to actions and behaviors which are probably wrong. We are going to place a lot of Band-Aids and do unnecessary work. Easy fixes often leave us wondering, "Why isn't this working? Why aren't these changes we've implemented getting us what we want?" One of the reasons might be the mindset you walked in with.

There are two types of mindsets. The first one is a fixed mindset. The fixed mindset says everything in life is fixed—your talent, your intelligence, your physical ability. It holds that these items are immovable and cannot be improved. In a fixed mindset, individuals work to protect their egos. They tend to process data, words, and body language from others in a self-centered way. They think most things are either about them or directed towards them. Failure is not an option for them—not because they work for NASA, but because it is a threat to their psyche. They will avoid challenges outside their strengths zones because they don't want to risk looking bad. When they do hit a stumbling block or an obstacle, they give up easily. They have a hard time dealing with it and usually refuse or ignore feedback from others. Finally, they can be threatened by the success of other people. They think they will look bad if others succeed.

I think some of us know somebody from medical school who behaved that way. They were the smartest folks in the room all through high school and undergrad. They were the "superstars." Then after they get to medical school and have a test where they might miss one or two questions, their world falls apart. If they continue to hold this mindset, these behaviors will continue into their clinical career.

The other mindset, the one that I want you to have, is a growth mindset, which is the belief that growth is possible. Intelligence can be improved. People believe talent exists, but skills can be developed. Physical ability can be improved; all it takes is effort. They will embrace a challenge and persist through the obstacles. They see effort as a path to mastery, learn from criticisms, and are inspired by others' successes.

To create change, you must have a growth mindset. You must say, "I don't have all the answers, but I can make this better. I can improve this process. I can improve on what's going on in my practice." If you possess a growth mindset, you will be able to say, "This isn't working, and I've got to figure out how to make it work. In fact, this may be my fault. Maybe I made the wrong decision, but we'll go ahead and make a different decision." Again, this goes back to effective decision-making. This is why a growth mindset is the starting point of effective leadership. Not only must you possess a growth mindset to create change, but your team must also have a growth mindset too. Eventually, you will want to change the "I" to "We" as in "*We* don't have all the answers, but *we* can make this better." This is where your leadership skills will make or break your practice. We will discuss leadership in a later chapter.

Sometimes, it takes time for us to change our mindset. Working at developing a growth mindset is the best place to start. We all carry some form of a fixed mindset with us. Recognizing that and attempting to change it will be the first step to making change. You can choose the mindset and the attitude, the way you think and feel. You can wake up every day and make that choice. And so I would ask you: which mindset, which attitude do you want? Do you want a fixed mindset or a growth mindset? Which mindset is going to be the best for you to possess as you try to have the practice you desire? I'll give you a hint—it's a growth mindset.

Once you've begun to develop a strong growth mindset, you are now able to assemble the pieces for delivering exemplary patient care. In the next chapter, we will examine the required parts to accomplish that.

Takeaways

> ➤ Your mindset—your attitude—will determine your success not only in your professional career but in life as well.
> ➤ You can choose the attitude or mindset you hold. Pick a growth mindset.
> ➤ A growth mindset is fundamental to being an effective change leader.

3

The Four Ps of
Exemplary Patient Care

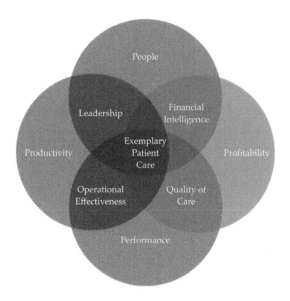

The goal of physician leaders is to ensure that their organization delivers exemplary patient care. It's an easy thing to say, but it is much more challenging to accomplish. As I began to work with other physician leaders, I developed a model that helps to focus the leader's attention on four key areas. I call it the Four Ps of Exemplary Patient Care: People, Productivity, Performance, and Profitability. With the goal of exemplary patient care, let's examine each area and discover how they contribute to exemplary patient care.

People

Healthcare organizations are service providers, and their real assets are their people and the knowledge, skills, and judgment they possess. It is peoples' knowledge and skills, combined thoughtfully and productively, that is the product being offered. The ability to diagnose, create a treatment plan, and provide the necessary follow-up to make sure the patient's ailment is treated correctly is the service the patient is purchasing from the organization. Naturally, we desire to find and work with the best, most talented people possible. Unfortunately, it is a little more complicated than that. Healthcare today is delivered as a team, and the physician leader must work diligently to assemble well-functioning teams. A strong leader understands how and why their people behave as they do. A strong leader will not only assign tasks and place people in the correct positions properly, but they will serve as a source of inspiration, be a mentor, and coordinate the responsibilities of those they lead. Ultimately, exemplary patient care begins with having the right people in the right places. That skill comes with leadership.

Productivity

Productivity is the quantity of work performed in a given time. How many phone calls are made in a day? How many patients are seen in an hour? How many bills are filed in a week? A strong physician leader knows and understands the many variables that come into play in an active practice. They know and see how each person's tasks and responsibilities affect and are affected by others within the organization. Physician leaders recognize and work to remove the roadblocks that hinder people in their daily tasks.

Creating a balanced scorecard that includes the right metrics is critical. Implement tracking as early as possible so that you have a good baseline. Keep the results public and visible to all employees and note changes in your metrics as you refine your operation.

Performance

Performance is a measure of the quality of care. Obtaining the right diagnosis at the right time and providing the right therapy at the best possible cost are just pieces of performance. These are more objective metrics the leader can use to determine the performance of the practice. What the patient feels and thinks is also important when considering performance. Subjective metrics, such as patient satisfaction scores, give insight into the care provided by the practice. How happy the patient is with the care provided will become more critical as the healthcare industry continues to change. Monitoring performance is challenging but necessary. Strong physician leadership skills are required to address this area.

Profitability

No matter which type of practice provides care—either for-profit, not-for-profit, or non-profit—cash flow is of utmost importance. The amount of money coming into the practice must at least equal the amount of money going out. Losing money makes it very difficult to stay in practice and keep the doors open to serve patients. Profitability is not a bad word. It simply means the practice is covering their costs to provide care. They have the capital to acquire newer, more efficient technologies. They have money to invest in the organization and continually improve it by focusing on the *People, Productivity*, and *Performance*. The physician leader needs a good, solid foundation in financial intelligence if the proper business decisions are to be made.

Exemplary Patient Care

With each decision, the physician leader should think about the four Ps. They should ask, "Do we have the right people? How well is the team working? What are the roadblocks they face? What can we do to make their jobs more efficient? How can we improve quality and reduce errors? What capital do we have available to invest? Where is the best place to invest that capital?" Having the right people working as efficiently as possible, doing their best work, while ensuring costs are at least equal in revenue, is the only way to provide exemplary patient care. Once you have all four pieces in place, you are equipped to provide exemplary patient care.

A culture of continuous process improvement is critical to ensuring all aspects of a process can be challenged in order to improve it regardless of the process, the owner of the process, or its stakeholders. A culture like this begins with a growth mindset, and the success of any change initiative is predicated upon the mindset and the culture of the leaders and organization.

Four Characteristics Required for Physician Leader

As the physician leader begins to understand and integrate the four Ps, they recognize how all four work together to create an environment in which exemplary patient care can be delivered.

Leadership

Having the proper leadership is key to the success of any practice. People may bring their skill sets and knowledge bases that will impact the effectiveness of the group. Still, it is the leadership that leverages that knowledge with the operational systems of the practice to create a highly productive practice. Leaders can see what others don't yet see and make the correct decisions in the face of an ever-changing industry. The leader must also make hard financial decisions as the practice changes. These critical decisions require solid financial intelligence.

Leadership is not only about having proper business knowledge, such as financial intelligence and operational know-how. It is also emotional intelligence. The leader must have the skills to know and understand how their people think and act. This is incredibly important as we begin to introduce change into the practice.

Operational Effectiveness

The ultimate goal of any practice is to be both highly productive while delivering the highest level of care to their patients. This requires both productivity and performance to be closely monitored and managed. The people of the organization are critical for a lean and effective practice. Their thoughts, ideas, and efforts are essential in order for a practice to succeed. It is the people working at not only the most efficient but at their best, which yields operational effectiveness. A highly effective operation works to create an environment that maintains the lowest costs, thus ensuring profitability.

Quality of Care

The performance of the organization is also critical to profitability. An organization that is delivering high-quality care works to help maintain the profitability of the practice. Patients will return and recommend others to a practice that consistently provides high-quality care. Demand for the practice's services increases and works to help maintain profitability. In turn, the profitably of the practice allows for the investment in newer technology, personnel, and other features that ensure the highest quality of performance and quality of care. Having a high-performing practice will help ensure patients are treated with the right therapy at the right time and for the right cost. This will ultimately raise the value of the practice, and it's profitability.

Every physician wants their patients to be treated quickly, correctly and accurately, and compassionately. Doing so will help the profitability of the practice by increasing patient satisfaction, word-of-mouth referrals, and the general regard of the practice in the community.

Financial Intelligence

Being profitable is more than a positive net income at the end of the fiscal period. Start thinking of financial performance not as how much cash you took out in a period, but as a metric showing how well all aspects of the four Ps collectively perform. It is a combination of the people of the organization and their decisions, coupled with the performance of the organization that yields a financially healthy practice. A good physician leader understands that the people of the organization make decisions that affect the profitability of the practice. Therefore, those decision-makers must have a sound and solid understanding of finance and accounting; they need financial intelligence. Operational effectiveness cannot be accomplished without an understanding of the cost accounting structure in place within the organization. When you make a change, evaluate the measured effect in your next financial statement.

When a physician leader understands and has in place the four Ps—Profitability, Performance, Productivity, and People—the practice is well suited to deliver exemplary patient care. The financial intelligence, the operational effectiveness, the quality of care provided, and the leadership of the practice support the four Ps. When all of these pieces are in place, exemplary patient care is the final result. Patients are cared for in an efficient, cost-effective, compassionate manner, which is the ultimate goal for any physician.

You'll notice most of the pieces of exemplary patient care are intangible, things we can't really touch. This is important because that's what service is. In the next chapter, we will examine the components of a service and how to define it.

Takeaways

- ➢ There are four aspects of exemplary patient care. Assemble all four to develop the practice you desire.
- ➢ You must have the right people.
- ➢ You must be profitable.
- ➢ You must have effective processes to provide quality care in an efficient manner.

4

Characteristics of Service

What is Service?

Unlike the manufacturing world, service can be a challenging concept to define. It is difficult to easily define the "widget" being delivered to the patient. A pharmacy can identify the drugs dispensed to a patient, but how does a physical therapist quantify the rehab given to a patient? How does a physician determine how much care a patient receives? These concepts are nebulous. To help us understand this concept, we will discuss four aspects of service that help define what service is.

The Aspects of Service

First, the service is **intangible**. It can be hard to physically see or feel the service being provided. The patient does feel it when we auscultate their lungs. They feel better when we provide pain medicine or antibiotics for an infection. However, these are facilitating goods—physical reminders of the service provided—but the actual improvement in their health is a bit more intangible. Just like services, products can also have facilitating services, such as an iPhone. The tangible iPhone has facilitating services such as phone calls, text messages, surfing the web, and watching videos on YouTube.

Second, there is **simultaneous production and consumption** of the service. When a physician examines a patient and arrives at a diagnosis, the service provided is produced and consumed at the same time by the patient.

Third, many services in healthcare are **in close proximity** to the consumer or patient. Fixing a broken bone, determining the source of an infection, and treating a heart attack or stroke are all things that have occurred very close to the patient, if not directly to them. There are some services, such as the interpretation of radiographic images, that occur away from the patient, but the patient still experiences the process of obtaining the image. Part of the service provided is in close proximity.

Finally, the service **cannot be inventoried**. We cannot walk into the back room of a clinic and pull a physician's service off the shelf. I'm sure many a hospital administer wishes this were true, but it's not. Providing a service is where we take the materials, the equipment, the people, the knowledge, the technology, and the facilities, and put all of those together to create the customer experience. We do that through our interaction with the patient and deliver services and their associated benefits, which results in specific feelings and judgments of the patient.

Again, What Is Service?

While a product is a tangible thing (like an iPhone, book, car, etc.), a service is an activity. It's a process or a set of actions or steps that involves the patient in some manner. It takes some inputs, combining them in such a way as to add value to the patient and achieve a desired output or outcome.

Another definition is that a service is the process of fulfilling a need for a patient. This process is probably larger than you may initially think. It occurs over a timeline from the first contact (before they ever set foot in your office) to the last part of the follow-up and billing.

Inputs of Service

Much like building a car, service providers will take other products—such as drugs, syringes, and suture—and combine them with the services of others (such as an EMR), then combine them with their processes to produce an outcome or experience for the patient. Materials, equipment, people, knowledge, technology, and facilities are all some standard inputs of a service. So from a company or service provider perspective, we think about our inputs, our processes, and our outputs. As a physician, my inputs might be that I need a certain number of nurses. I also need a certain amount of rooms to see patients. The clinic should be open for specific hours. Certain processes or steps should also be established. For example, a process might be getting the patient's appointment scheduled, getting them to the clinic and into a room, examining them, and prescribing therapy. Then out the door they go. Each organization has a unique way of combining these inputs and crafting outcomes and experiences for their patients.

Outputs of Service

Outputs in a service are more nebulous and complex than that of the manufacturing industries. The **product** of a service company is one part benefit to the patient, another how the patient feels, and partially the judgments of the patient. The **benefit** your service offers is the very reason the patient chose your practice. It's the gains they receive from seeing you. The emotions the patient experiences might include love, joy, surprise, anger, shame, fear, and sadness. Your process must manage these emotions as best as possible. Their judgments are their conscious and unconscious assessment of the quality of the care you provided. These judgments ultimately influence their intentions to continue to have you be their doctor or move on to someone else. As we consider the service we provide, we must remember there are two different perspectives to consider—that of the organization and the patients.

The Customer Perspective

The customer experience is how your patient interprets the service or process. It's their personal and direct interpretation of what you did—their participation in what you did. It's their journey through the process and all the touchpoints along the way. Since this is highly personal and individualized, no two patients will likely ever have the exact same experience. They may have close experience and similar outcomes, but each one will be slightly different.

The patient experience will be influenced by the degree of personal interaction and intimacy in the process. The responsiveness of your practice. The flexibility of your process and how valued they feel by your organization. Their experience is heavily influenced by the courtesy and competency of your people. Finally, don't forget your patients will likely interact with other patients of your practice. That interaction will also influence their perception of the service.

Why Should You Manage Your Service?

It's not easy managing a service, but it is imperative if you hope to deliver exemplary patient care. To help illustrate why developing this foundation of knowledge and skill set is essential, let's consider its impact.

It's better for your patients. Providing the right service to the right patient at the right time is the goal of every physician. Designing a process that helps ensure that becomes a reality solves your patient's problems. Once you understand that every patient visits you with different expectations and perceptions of the value you offer, the more apt you are at meeting and exceeding those expectations.

A well-operating process is also good for your people. Staff will have a higher quality of work-life when they know they are delivering the best care possible. Satisfied patients are easier to deal with, thus making work for the staff easier. They then become more engaged and take pride in what they do.

Having a well designed and operating process improves your organization because patients will return and brag about you in the marketplace. More efficient processes will lead to lower costs and higher revenues, thus improving profitability. Today's profit becomes capital for investment in the company tomorrow. That investment can become a competitive advantage in the marketplace, further benefiting the organization.

Two Perspectives When Designing a Process

A common challenge that affects anyone who works in a service industry is that they see things from an internal point of view. They see how the process works from combining the materials, resources, talent, and people to create the service for the patient. We are typically experts in the service we provide. The problem arises when that's all we consider.

We try to manage the people, resources, and materials (and even the patient at times) to ensure the process works well. However, even though that makes sense to us, we often miss the point of view of the patient. They see the service as one that is received rather than provided. Our patients aren't that concerned with the management of the resources of the practice nor the cost of the care (unless they're paying for it). They don't care if your people meet targets and metrics. What they care about is how they feel and if they are treated well and properly. Did you solve their problem?

As you design your process, you will want to be aware of both the internal (inside-out) view as well as the external (outside-in) viewpoint. You will want to align these two viewpoints as much as possible. Value might be delivered through the processes and service, but the real value—that perceived by the patient—is located in their experience and outcomes.

Let's consider a hospital's and patient's point of view as they examine the same service. A seventy-two-year-old patient has a painful hip and cannot ambulate well. They must use a walker, and stairs are difficult, making portions inaccessible to them. The patient sees an orthopedic surgeon who recommends surgical replacement. The patient arrives at the hospital and undergoes surgery to fix the problem. Both the patient and hospital recognize the hip requires replacement; however, how they determine the customer experience might be different.

The healthcare providers might view the process as taking the inputs of the OR staff, surgeon, anesthesia, equipment, PT, and other post-operative care, and combining them to successfully replace the hip. Their output is a hip that has been replaced in the patient. For most providers, this is how we see the process.

Your Perspective		
Input	Processes	Output
MDs, RNs, surgeon, anesthesia, OR room, floor room, equipment, PT	Diganosis, treatment, surgery, post-operative care plan	Hip is replaced

However, the patient might have a different perspective. Yes, they do want their hip replaced, but their perspective doesn't include all the inputs as the health organization sees them. Instead, their experience is influenced by the empathetic care they receive, how quickly they can get home after the operation, and ultimately if their pain has been relieved and they can ambulate once again.

Their Perspective		
Experience	The Service	Their Benefits
Empathetic care, quick and proper care, easy-to-understand instructions	Arthritic hip replaced	Pain is relieved; Able to ambulate without pain; Resume normal life activities

Well-designed services aim to align these two perspectives as best as possible. The best way to align them is to begin with the patient's perspective and ask the following questions:

> How does the patient feel throughout the process? Do they feel like a unique person or just another work order?
> How easy are the instructions to understand?
> Has the real problem been solved for the patient?
> Have we outlined the benefits of the service delivered?

In the next chapter, we will look at some tools we can use to begin to understand and then improve our processes.

Takeaways

> Know your processes.
> Diagram them to know them.
> Go through the process as a provider *and* as a patient.

5

What's Your Process?

When a patient seeks your services, they are buying more than the essential elements of what you provide. They are looking for something much more significant and more intangible. Just as you might compare all theme parks to Disney, your patients will have the same idea about service. At Disney, they go beyond providing you a room, bed, places to eat, etc. They provide an experience that they have carefully designed. Part of that experience comes from their people. Disney is very clear in the concept of their service and what they must do to meet their customers' expectations. It's easy for those working in the service industry to lose sight of the customer because we focus on the inputs and processes. Developing a service concept will help you and your staff stay focused on why you're in business—the patient.

Understanding the Service Concept

The service concept is incredibly important to your organization if you are to deliver exemplary patient care. It's often poorly understood and less shared or articulated by the people providing the service. To be effective, the service concept must be shared and articulated, communicated.

So what is the service concept? It's a solid understanding of what you do and why you do it. It's referred to as the organizing idea, or as I call it: your mission and purpose. When we break down the service concept, it has three essential parts. The **what** you are doing, which is the service the customer purchases. The **how** you provide that service by combing the inputs via processes to craft the service. Finally, the **why,** which are the benefits of the service the customer received. The why comes from elements of the customer experience and the outcomes they receive.

As a leader of a service organization, one of your primary duties is to craft and share your mission and purpose, your service concept, with your people. This is a critical first step in designing a service that delights the patient. Get this wrong, and you'll miss the mark on down the road.

Your Mission and Purpose

An organizing idea, or mission and purpose, is a powerful way to remind yourself and your staff what the patient is buying. It will help you to focus your talents, resources, and capital on designing a process that genuinely delivers the patient care your patients desire.

To begin to develop and understand your mission and purpose statement, follow these rules to help you craft a powerful and easily shared and understood message.

> ➤ What is it you are delivering to the patient?
> ➤ Why are you doing it? This must be from the patient's point of view too.
> ➤ The statement must be based in their world for their benefit.
> ➤ It must be written down.
> ➤ It must be as short as possible. If you get too wordy, people will get lost.
> ➤ What's the value? Maximize the benefits, minimize the costs to the patient and the organization.

Keep in mind your service concept isn't a business model, a vision statement, a mission statement, an idea, a brand, a service promise, or a business proposition. Instead, it's clearly defining what you do, how you do it, and why you do it.

An example of a mission and purpose would be my mission and purpose, which is to help physicians have the practice they desire by raising their business intelligence through education. The **what**? The experience. I try to make them very easy to use and understand concepts and courses and books, and the outcome that I hope to have as a physician who understands and possesses business intelligence and is, therefore, able to create the practice they desire. The **why**? I want them to enjoy their careers and not feel like they are swimming upstream in their businesses. The **how**? I do this through online education, books, seminars, and consulting.

You should know what it is you're doing, why you're doing it, how you're doing it, who's doing it, and what the benefits or outcomes are that you desire for the patient. These are important in defining your unique service. It may seem like this is rudimentary or elementary, but you need to begin with the basics to understand what it is we do and why we're doing it. This will help you stay on task (we'll discuss process improvement later." As Jim Rohn once said, "Things that are easy to do are easy not to do." It's my opinion many of the issues physicians face in their clinics are simple matters which are often overlooked. The problem occurs when we pile simple problems upon other simple problems and don't take the care or expend the energy to dissect them down to the parts.

As we begin to define our processes, the most important source of information that will guide our decision-making is the perspective of the patient. To understand that, we must first connect with them. In the next chapter, we will examine ways you can connect with your patients and gather the information that will help you design a system they want.

Takeaways

> - Define your **what**. What is it that you do?
> - Define your **why**. Why do you do what you do? Who does it benefit, and how?
> - Define **how** you do what you do.
> - Team alignment on your mission and purpose will aid in creating a culture of continuous improvement.

6

Connect With Your Patient

In this chapter, we are going to talk about connecting with your customers. Connecting with your customer begins with understanding who your customer is. Who exactly is your customer? A customer can be many things for you. They can be the patient. A customer might also be the hospital or ambulatory surgery center. Your customer might be another physician. Your customer might be health plans or employers. They might be high-value or low-value customers. They can be inside or outside for your organization.

For each process, the second step to improving it is to identify who the customer is. In your process overall—in your clinic overall—you may have a bunch of different processes. Some of those processes may have an external customer. Others may have an internal customer. They may have a large, high-value customer, or they may have a low value one, but you need to identify who those customers are for each specific process. For example, the billing office has processes that serve you, an internal customer, as well as external customers, such as a third-party payer. Once you've identified the customer, you can then examine how the service flows.

Service is always a two-way street. Information flows between you and your customer, and that information is essential because it allows you to adapt to the needs of the patient. The exchange of information between you and the patient leads to change. I'm not only talking about clinical information but service process information as well. The sharing of that information not only helps you improve the service provided but will lead to changes in what the customer expects. To use the information correctly, we need to understand what our process is and look for ways to keep information flowing between the patient and us. When we do that, we can then manage our customer's expectations. After all, we aim to develop and provide services that have high customer satisfaction.

And satisfaction is their overall assessment of their perceptions of the service. There are three main components of our process, their experiences, and their outcomes. We're attempting to strike a balance between their expectations and their perceptions, experiences, and outcomes. We want to understand what it is, so once we begin to understand how they perceive the service in terms of experiences and outcomes, we can then, as we said with that two-way communication, begin to shape and mold and modify those expectations of your patient. As they go through our service, their expectations will lead to their perceptions.

Managing their expectations is what we're trying to do. We want to be able to figure out how we can balance expectations and perceptions. I'm not advocating we manipulate them, but rather we want them to have reasonable expectations so they can perceive the service properly. So like we said, expectations through the service lead to the perceptions.

The important thing to realize is that organizations may have different customers throughout the same service. Also, notice that service is a two-way process with the exchange of information. This flow of information between you and the patient is critical because it will lead to changes in the service provided. It also leads to changes in the patient's expectations of your service.

Managing Customer Expectations and Satisfaction

It's important to manage the expectations of your patients. If done properly, you can ensure their satisfaction. Satisfaction is their overall assessment of their perceptions of the service. Your process ends with their experiences, their outcomes. Their expectations influence their perceptions. Their perceptions influence their expectations. The service you provide affects both expectations and perceptions.

Many organizations assume they know what the patient wants. Often, professionals fall into the trap of thinking they know what the patient wants because they are, after all, the experts. Understanding what satisfies and delights your patients is something that must be continually investigated and addressed. As technology and patient populations change in your practice, your patients will change too. Don't think what worked to please them five years ago will work tomorrow.

Your patient's expectations form part of how they will experience your service, which influences their perceptions and, ultimately, their satisfaction. Your goal should be to understand their expectations and perceptions of your service so you can influence their satisfaction.

Gaps occur because of a mismatch between expectations and service exists, or a mismatch between perceptions and service. The first gap, a mismatch between expectation and service, occurs when your service has been inappropriately specified, designed, or implemented. It's also possible the patient has the wrong expectations because of poor understanding on their part.

The second gap, a service and perception mismatch, occurs when the incorrect service is provided. The patient might also incorrectly perceive the service, their experience, or the outcomes.

Influencers of Expectations

As you are designing your processes, keep in mind many variables will influence the expectations of your patients. Some will be under your direct control, while others will not.

One variable is the price of your service and higher- and lower-priced services. There is a correlation between the price and the level of expectation of quality. A lower price leads to lower expectations. Imagine having a cheeseburger at McDonald's compared to Red Robin. First, the price is considerably different between the two establishments. The service and the experience are substantially different as well. Your expectations and perceptions when you walk into either one of those are going to be different.

If you examine how McDonald's and Red Robin operate, you will quickly notice they differ on several points such as price, their marketing, and their reputation. They count on your previous experiences to bring you back into their establishment. They know there are alternatives in the marketplace and are trying to position themselves properly in the customer's mind. You should be doing the same thing in your practice.

The price of your service will affect your patients' expectations. Often, this information is known to the patient, and more than likely, they might not care unless they have a high deductible plan or poor insurance. More and more patients are expecting to have a good idea of what the service provided will cost them. This knowledge will directly affect their expectations and perceptions of your service. A higher price tag will raise their expectations of you and your service.

Another variable is the alternatives you face in the marketplace. Just as there are several places I can go to get a burger, there are several places where your patients can go to get surgery or treatment for their ailments. Whether it be competing physicians, other healthcare professionals, or other clinics, the patient will compare you to your competitors.

The third variable is marketing. How are you marketing yourself? What's the image that you're portraying and getting out there into the marketplace? How you sell your service to the public also carries with it information they will use to formulate their expectations. Are the ads and other marketing materials done cheaply, or are they high quality? Be mindful of the message you send to the public. The quality and cleanliness of your facilities is another form of marketing many clinics neglect.

Another essential variable is your reputation and word-of-mouth referral. What's the word on the street say about you? If the patient comes to your clinic after hearing everyone rave about you, their expectations will be quite high.

Their previous experiences with you also have a significant impact. After a few good experiences, patients will forgive a bad experience; they will mark it as a one-off and overlook it. The goal is to always deliver great care and service, but there are times when that can be challenging, and mistakes are made. Be careful not to rely on previous experiences to forgive one bad event, either. Don't take the customer for granted.

Their attitude and mood is another variable influencing their perceptions and expectations. How your patient is feeling impacts their perceptions. What you say and how you and your staff behave can influence and alter those feelings. Teach yourself and your staff to be mindful of the cues your patients are providing. If they're hurting or are in a foul mood, that can adversely affect their perception of their experience.

Finally, the confidence you display is the final important variable. If you don't act confident, your patient won't have confidence in you either. Don't fake it either. They will see through any false portrayal of confidence.

The Zone of Tolerance

Patients have a zone of tolerance based upon their expectations, which are influenced by those items discussed earlier in this chapter. If you desire to influence and manage their perceptions, you must understand and know their expectations. Managing the patient's perceived quality during your process is a dynamic activity. Expectations lead to perceptions, so design your process to influence their satisfaction.

Your patient's satisfaction will vary throughout your care delivery process. However, research has shown their overall satisfaction and their final perception is heavily influenced by how they felt during their peaks—good and bad—and at the end. Of note, it is their final experience of the process that will ultimately lead to their perception. In other words, always end on a good note and know what's important to the patient to make them feel they've ended on a good note. Most patients desire explanations and answers. Take the time to provide those.

Expectations Levels

1. **Ideal** - the best service possible.
2. **Feasible ideal** - the level of service commiserate with the price and industry standard.
3. **Desirable** - the standard the patient wants.
4. **Deserved** - the level they ought to receive based upon costs.
5. **Minimum tolerated** - the minimum level of service the patient will expect.
6. **Intolerable** - below the standards of what a patient should receive.

Identify those points which dramatically affect their expectations either negatively or positively. The middle ground between these two areas is the zone of tolerance. It's the area in which your patients will be satisfied but not delighted nor dissatisfied. If you operate within the zone, you'll have a satisfied patient. Your job is to figure out how you can enhance the experience and delight them while avoiding those aspects that will dissatisfy them.

Design a system, a process that operates within the zone of tolerance.

A handful of factors influences overall satisfaction.

- The peaks (best and worst) experiences
- How they felt at the end of the service

Therefore, design your processes with the end in mind.

An Example

Let's take a look at what I'm talking about. Hypothetically, say that the top line is a fully satisfied patient. The bottom line is a fully dissatisfied patient. The second line from the top is the upper limit of their zone of tolerance, while the next line down is the lower limit of their zone of tolerance. Anytime the patient is between these two lines the patient is okay. Anything outside the area between these two lines means they're dissatisfied. (Fig. 6.1)

Fig. 6.1

On surveys, a patient might describe your staff and clinic as "They're friendly, the staff is friendly, they recognize me, and they're empathetic." They are going to be satisfied with that. But they're walking in to expect to wait ten minutes, and are expecting meaningful explanations and consideration. But if they wait twenty minutes or receive the wrong diagnosis, or maybe it's a cold room, or even cold personnel in terms of attitude, the patient is going to be dissatisfied, and that will fall below that zone of tolerance.

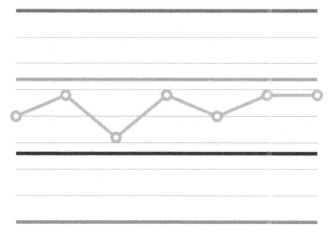

Fig. 6.2

Let's say you have a patient, and they're waiting ten minutes to start with. The staff is friendly, but the patient is expecting that. The physician is on time. And then the staff and physician provide excellent care. Instructions are given and understood. The checkout is quick and easy, and follow-up is completed. Now you've met all the metrics there. These are the things they expect, so they're going to walk away satisfied. (Fig. 6.2)

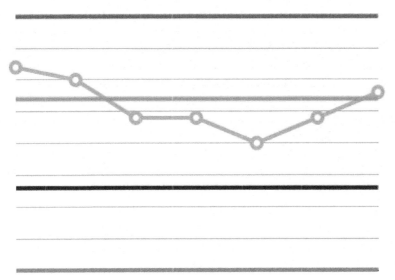

Fig. 6.3

Now, let's say we designed a system, and they wait less than ten minutes. The staff is friendly. The physician's on time. The staff and the physician provide great care, instructions are given and understood, checkout is easy, and the follow-up is completed promptly, as promised. You'll see that a majority of the patients' experiences were above their expectations, their zone of tolerance. That happened because you designed the process that way. (Fig. 6.3)

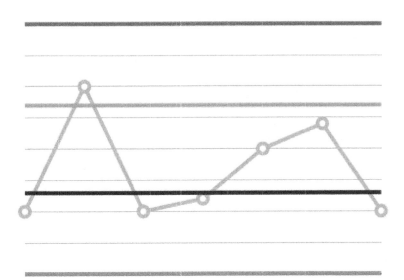

Fig. 6.4

Now, this is the way most physicians' offices work. They wait for more than ten minutes. The staff is friendly. That's great. But the physician is late. The staff was cool or hurried, and the physician seemed rushed. I got some instructions and understood what they were talking about. Checkout was easy, but no one ever followed up with me. And right there, that's how you develop an unsatisfied patient who will probably eventually leave, or not refer new patients or other family members to you. (Fig. 6.4)

Patients ask their friends and families, and if they know doctors, they ask, "Who should I go to? Who would you recommend?" And that word of mouth is incredibly important. The satisfaction your patient's going to walk away with is going to be determined by the peaks and troughs of how they feel and, most importantly, that last interaction. But you have to sit down and design a process where you are managing those expectations. So you've got to understand, establish, and manage the expectations of your patient.

Now, some factors can affect your quality. A number of those would be their access to you, the aesthetics of your facility, the helpfulness and availability of your staff, the concern and empathy demonstrated and displayed, the cleanliness of the space, the comfort of the patient areas, the communication between you and the patient, the commitment of your staff, the competency of you and your staff, your flexibility, friendliness, and the integrity and responsiveness of your staff. These are all factors that can affect the quality (or perceived quality) of your service.

A Herzberg-Like Model of Service

I don't know if any of you are familiar with Herzberg, but he was a gentleman who did some stuff in organizational behavior many decades ago in terms of leadership. Several decades ago, somebody took a look at his model of leadership, which says there are hygiene and motivating factors that will motivate an employee to work, and applied it to the service industry. And they say there are hygiene or modifying or pleasing factors rather than motivating ones. In Herzberg's model, he said there are some things you have to have in place to have a motivated place—an employee. And then there are things that, if you put into place, will motivate them even further. He said the things you have to have in place would work to remove dissatisfaction, but if you want to motivate employees, you've got to take care of the things that dissatisfy them, and then add some things that satisfy them—or motivate, I should say.

The same thing happens when we're talking about a service. Dissatisfaction is not the opposite of satisfaction or delight. It just means that they are dissatisfied. There are two types of factors: hygiene factors, things that need to be in place to satisfy. And if they are absent, these factors will dissatisfy the customer.

The service aspects listed previously can be gathered into four distinct groups. Using a model similar to Herzberg's model of leadership and employee satisfaction, we can determine which areas or aspects we should focus on for the maximum impact.

Before we delve into that, let's discuss an important distinction or definition. Satisfaction and dissatisfaction are not opposites. Rather, dissatisfaction is the absence of satisfaction. Also, like Herzberg's model, there are hygiene and enhancing factors.

Hygiene factors are those factors that need to be in place to satisfy the patient. If they are absent, they will dissatisfy the patient. Enhancing factors are those factors that delight the patient if they are present. However, if they are absent, they likely do not lead to dissatisfaction.

And then there are enhancing factors; these factors can delight if present, but if absent likely do not lead to dissatisfaction. That's where the Herzberg-ish model comes into play. You have to get the hygiene factors in there to satisfy, and if they're not there, you're going to dissatisfy them. But if you want to delight, you need to add them. But if they're not there, they may not, more than likely, lead to dissatisfaction.

The Data

So let's look at the data. When we're looking at attentiveness and dissatisfaction, if you're attentive, you delight them. If you're responsive, it's about a 50/50 mix. So if you provide good care, and they believe you care about them, that will delight them. Being unavailable will lead to a big dissatisfaction, not being reliable, not doing what you do, saying what you do, not having integrity. Big dissatisfiers.

I don't know about you, but I remember several times when my mother called me and said, "The doctor didn't follow up with me like they said they would," and I had to call them, and they acted like I was bothering them. Well, guess what? That's a huge dissatisfier. And it just screams unreliable and lack of integrity. Friendliness doesn't have to be there, but if it is, it truly delights—courtesy, competency, functionality, commitment, access, flexibility, aesthetics, cleanliness. Those are the data points, and those are the things, if we look at that, we can say if these things are present, they're going to be dissatisfied. But if we don't have these things there, those are going to lead to a dissatisfied patient. So we've got to work on responsiveness, availability, reliability, and integrity. Maybe we need to work on communication; maybe we need to work on functionality.

So if we look at the potential to delight and the potential to dissatisfy and we put them in a nice little grid, things that have a high potential to dissatisfy are going to be availability, reliability, functionality, and integrity. And the things that would have a high potential to delight and a high potential to dissatisfy are going to be your communication responsiveness and competency.

Things that have a low potential to delight and dissatisfy are going to be the comfort and aesthetics of your service, or where they're experiencing the service. And then something that's going to have a high potential to delight but a low potential to dissatisfy is going to be the flexibility, attentiveness, courtesy, and friendliness of your staff and clinic.

These are the hygiene factors. They are the enhancers you're going to want to do. Attentiveness and courtesy are going to enhance satisfaction. Responsiveness, communication, and competency are critical for your practice to have. Things that are going to be neutral are going to be comfort, aesthetics, plus, minus. But you have to have integrity, reliability, and availability, and then focus on the critical ones, and then come down to the enhancers. As a suggestion, I would spend your time on comfort and aesthetics.

Dissatisfiers are responsiveness, availability, reliability, and integrity. Note the absence of these aspects offers only dissatisfaction, and their presence does not delight the patient. If you want to prevent dissatisfaction, you must be responsive, available, reliable, and operate with integrity.

Delighters are attentiveness, responsiveness, care, friendliness, and courtesy. Oddly, these are not necessary to satisfy the patient but will delight them if you do these. So be attentive, friendly, show you care, and be courteous regardless of how they are treating you and your staff.

Factors That Affect Your Quality

There are many factors you will want to consider as you determine what is important to your patients and what you will need to pay attention to.

➤ **Access:** How easy is it for them to reach your location?

➤ **Aesthetics:** How pleasing to the eye is the appearance of your area?

➤ **Helpfulness, concern, and empathy:** What is the impression your staff gives to the patient? Do they appear to be caring and interested in the patient?

➤ **Availability:** Are you available to provide care when they need you to?

➤ **Cleanliness:** How clean are your facilities? Have you invested capital into the infrastructure?

➤ **Comfort:** How comfortable is it to rest and wait in your facilities? What is the environment like?

➤ **Communication:** How well and often do you communicate with the patient? What sort of information do you share with them? How do you communicate? How do they want to be communicated with?

➤ **Competency:** Are you and your staff competent in the care you provide?

➤ **Flexibility:** Are you able to deliver different types of care at different times?

➤ **Friendliness:** Are you and your staff friendly?

➤ **Integrity:** Do you have integrity? Do you do what you say? Do you practice what you preach?

➤ **Responsiveness:** How quickly do you respond to patient inquiries?

The chart above shows the ability to either delight or dissatisfy the patient.

Attentiveness	Delight	
Responsiveness	Delight	Dissatisfy
Care	Delight	Dissatisfy
Availability		
Reliability		Dissatisfy
Integrity		Dissatisfy
Courtesy	Delight	
Communication	Delight	Dissatisfy
Functionality		Dissatisfy
Commitment	Delight	
Access	Delight	Dissatisfy
Flexibility	Delight	Dissatisfy
Aesthetics and cleanliness	Delight	Dissatisfy

What to Focus On?

Knowing what to focus on as you attempt to delight your patient is important. Sometimes, knowing what to avoid is easier to begin with. If you want to **dissatisfy** your patients, do the following:

- ➢ Be slow to respond
- ➢ Don't be available
- ➢ Don't be reliable
- ➢ Don't have integrity
- ➢ Don't communicate
- ➢ Don't be competent

If you are currently doing any of those things with your patients, you are likely dissatisfying them. I'd venture a guess they aren't real happy with your clinic. Doing the opposite of these things will not delight the patient either. It will merely satisfy them. To **delight** the patient, do the following:

- ➢ Be attentive to them
- ➢ Be responsive
- ➢ Care about them and demonstrate it
- ➢ Be friendly
- ➢ Communicate with them

The ones you must have in place: availability, reliability, integrity, functionality. Followed by responsiveness, communication, and competency. To enhance the experience, be attentive, care for them, be courteous, friendly, and flexible. The lowest yield items are comfort and aesthetics. Spend your money wisely.

Getting the Data

So how do you get this data? Well, you can do questionnaires and surveys as well as customer or patient advisory panels. You can even ask new and past customers (send them surveys) why they left the clinic. You can even have a complaint and a compliment analysis system. If somebody files a complaint, make certain that it's about the process and not necessarily about the individual. Now sometimes, the process involves the person or persons. And if there's a real problem there, then you need to address it.

But first, I would always approach all complaints by taking a look at what the problem is with the process. If you can't find one, then it could be the person. But focus on figuring out what the problem is, the complaint the patient had about the process.

So think about what will delight your customers, and make sure to utilize:

➤ Questionnaires and surveys
➤ Patient advisory panel
➤ New and past patient surveys
➤ Complaint and compliment analysis

After you've developed a connection to your patients, you can then begin to craft your service-scape. We will take a deeper look at what the servicescape is in the next chapter.

Takeaways

➤ Connecting with your patients goes beyond making the diagnosis. It's understanding them.
➤ Their expectations will determine their satisfaction.
➤ Your systems don't have to be perfect as long as you stay within their zone of tolerance.
➤ You can influence their expectations by focusing on the proper dissatisfiers and delighters.

7 | The Servicescape

In healthcare, the patient experiences the service we provide in a physical environment, whether that be an exam room, waiting room, OR room, or hospital room. The environment the patient receives the service we provide—the servicescape—is essential and greatly influences their perception of the quality of care we provide. The servicescape also goes beyond the physical aspects of a building or room.

The term **servicescape** is an all-encompassing concept used to describe what the patient will experience in the physical environment. The servicescape comprises everything the patient will see, touch, feel, smell, hear—these physical aspects of the environment impact the patient's experience. Their senses provide them clues as to what to expect from you and your clinic.

As you build your servicescape, carefully consider the odors, the music, the texture of the chairs, any noise, etc., in your waiting room. Your patients will take the "data" perceived from their senses and use them to build their experience. Consider what you experience at any Disney property. Their servicescape is a vital part of your experience and is part of what you pay for. The service they're providing, from the roller coasters to the shows to the costumed characters, is contained within their carefully designed and maintained servicescape. Step foot on a Disney property and you will quickly see how the servicescape supports and is integral to the service—the experience—they deliver. I'm not saying that we need to make every patient extremely happy as if they were at

Disneyland, but I do think we can have a dramatic impact upon how they experience our care in our servicescape. Designing a servicescape with the patient in mind will go a long way towards maximizing their experience and satisfaction.

The Customer Experience Statement

Before we begin to design our patient experience, we must define the experience we want the patient to have. Put yourself in their shoes and consider the experience and outcomes you think they might desire. Write down all emotions they should feel as a result of the experience and benefits of your service. It might be joy, fear, compassion, etc.

A great starting point as you design your servicescape is, to begin with, a customer experience statement. Define the experience you want the patient to have as they receive service from you. Include all the emotions they should feel as a result of the experience and benefits of the care you provide because it's essential to remember the power of emotion.

The Power of Emotion

Humans are emotional creatures. As much as we think we are rational beings making rational decisions, we cannot escape our emotional natures. Emotions drive our decisions. We want to believe we are rational, but all of our decisions are emotional. Our limbic nervous system overrules any rational decision-making. As emotions drive our decisions, our analytical brain searches for reasons to justify the emotion we feel. Our responses to feelings are swift and powerful—and often permanent, becoming very hard to change.

It's important to understand that we humans are emotional creatures, even those of us who don't think we are. We do possess all of these emotions, and we feel them to some extent. The problem is the power of emotion, and the influence of emotions is incredibly crucial because emotions drive decisions.

The seven primary emotions are:

> Joy
> Surprise
> Love
> Fear
> Anger
> Shame
> Sadness

As physicians, we deal with patients in one or many of those emotional states. Some are surprised. Some are fearful of what's about to happen. Some are angry that they are ill. They might be sad. Occasionally they'll feel joy when we share the results of tests or procedures. They should always feel love. We need to be aware their emotions can get tangled, especially if we operate in a servicescape that we didn't design. Their irritation and anger with the facility might be transferred to us if we aren't careful. We want our patients to have a positive emotional experience even when they face painful or stressful situations.

Keep in mind the permanence of our emotions and experiences. I have many examples in my personal life where I might hear something, see something, or smell something that brings back a memory to the forefront of my mind. For me, the smell of alcohol swabs takes me back to the hospital ward as a child when I was ill with pneumonia. I can still feel the sterility of the environment as well as the compassion of the staff. I'm sure you have your own experiences too. We help shape those memories and experiences for our patients, but we must do so purposefully by designing our servicescape properly.

Front-Office or Back-Office?

The other part we must consider when designing our servicescape is the front-office versus back-office processes. Front-office processes are those things that the patient comes to you for. You'll interact directly with the patient face-to-face, over the telephone, or even over the internet. Our back-office processes are those that the patient never sees. Whether it's building the chart or billing the proper fees, submitting the claim, etc., these are things they never witness but are essential. And when they go wrong, they impact their patient experience.

Often, we only focus on the front-office, patient-facing processes, but we have to be aware that both locations impact the customer's experience. As we begin to design the experience (the servicescape), there are many different methods we can use, which we'll discuss in the next chapter.

Takeaways

> Understanding your servicescape will allow you to control their emotions.
> Start with a customer service experience statement to help you determine the experience you want them to have.
> Understand the power of their emotions on their decisions, expectations, and satisfaction.

8

Tools to Design Your Servicescape

In the previous chapter, we discussed the servicescape and the importance of designing it thoughtfully. If done correctly, we can influence our patient's perception of our care. In this chapter, we will discuss a few tools you can use to help you understand and design your servicescape. The tools we will examine are the customer journey map, the walk-through audit, emotion mapping, and the customer experience analysis.

We will be mapping out the touchpoints between ourselves and the patient. Our front-office processes (those face-to-face, telephone, internet, and remote interactions) and our back-office processes (assembling the chart, billing the proper fee) are all things we will examine.

The first step is to determine and document the state of the process—the "as-is" state. This should be defined and documented by *all* the stakeholders engaged in the process. Once the "as-is" state is determined, the "to-be," or desired process, is developed by the same stakeholders. This step should address all waste, all pain points, all performance gaps—all non-value-added steps in the "as-is" process. During the development of the desired process, the stakeholders should be examining each step in the process for elimination, automation, or combining the step with another.

Design the Experience

Let's say we have a patient coming to our clinic for a mammo-gram (I'm using my wife's latest experience as an example). She had to find parking, then find Admissions to check in with the receptionist, sit in the waiting room, be escorted to the ultra-sound unit, sit in that waiting area, have the ultrasound, discuss the results with the radiologist, and then find the way back to the parking lot. That is an example of the customer journey and how we map that out. (Fig. 8.1)

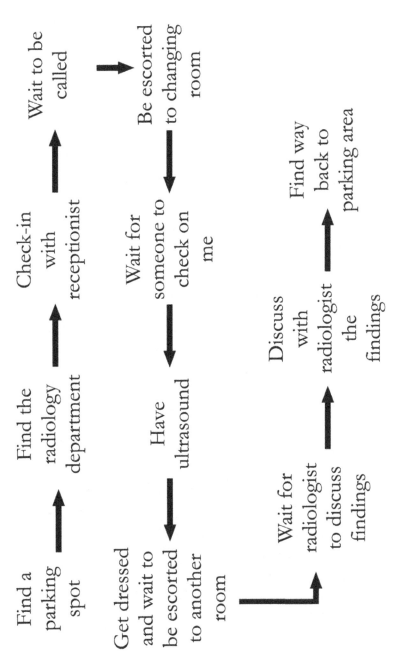

Fig. 8.1

Customer Journey Mapping

With a patient journey map, we will map out the touchpoints between you, your staff, your clinic, and the patient. It can begin at whatever point you'd like, whether that is the initial phone call or once they arrive in the parking lot. It then maps out the patient's journey through your service, stopping at each touchpoint and decision point they might make.

What is is like to find parking? Is it easy to find Admissions? Where is the waiting area? Is it comfortable? What are your senses telling you about it? Were you escorted to the room? How did you feel when talking with the physician, etc.?

Walk-Through Audits

A walk-through audit is a great way to gain the patient's perspective of your service. You, other staff, or consultants can act as a surrogate patient, similar to a mystery shopper. It's best to use someone your staff won't recognize so that they will be on their usual behavior, not their "best" behavior.

As the consultant experiences your process, they will make notes of their thoughts and feelings. Before they begin their audit, you might provide them a series of questions you would like answers to. Perhaps you have an idea of where issues exist in your process and would like confirmation. Often, my clients are surprised by the results. They are frequently close in their assumptions but discover things they didn't think of or didn't know were issues. This can be an excellent way of figuring out where exactly the experience might be less than optimal. Using a mystery patient will be a useful tool for you to identify problems in your process from the patient's point of view.

With an audit, you will also be able to determine if the issues are front-office or back-office and how they affect the overall process. With that knowledge in hand, you'll be improving your processes and exceed your patient's expectations.

Emotion Mapping

Emotion mapping is an extension of the customer journey map, but we take the map one step further. After you've mapped the experience and noted the experiences either you or the mystery patient felt, you will be able to gain insight into how you might need to adjust the servicescape to craft the emotional experience you desire for your patients.

Examination of the results should prompt questions as you review the data. Were you frustrated when trying to find parking? Confused when trying to find the office? Welcomed when checking in? Anxious while waiting? How did the physician make you feel? My wife's emotion map is provided as an example. (Fig. 8.1)

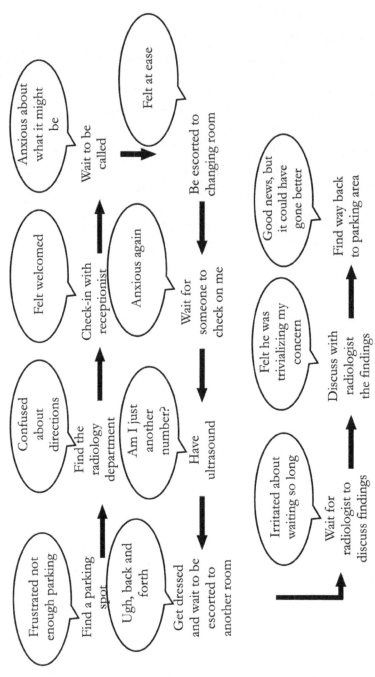

Fig. 8.2

Capturing the emotions of the patients will arm you with powerful data. Once you've identified the feelings of the patient of the process in the current state, you can then begin to change it to elicit the emotions you desire.

Do they get frustrated walking in from the parking lot? What difficulties might your patient population face as they traverse your lot? If you're in a medical office building, is it easy to find? How much time do they spend waiting in various areas?

Customer Experience Analysis

The final step is to put all of these pieces together to create one all-encompassing map. We combine the data from the journey map, the walk-through audit, and the emotion map. We will create one large diagram of the patient experience in the process. This can take quite a bit of work, but if you do it right, it can set you apart from your competition in terms of designing the type of process (the system) that you want your patient to experience.

After we have connected with the patient, crafted our servicescape, and walked through the process, we need to build a visual representation of the experience that can be shared with those people involved in the process. To do that, we need to develop a flowchart or service map. In the next chapter, we will examine how to build and use flow charts and service maps.

Takeaways

> ➤ Design your service by beginning with the patient's perspective.
> ➤ Use a journey map to understand how your patient experiences your service.
> ➤ An emotion map can help identify positive and negative influencing touchpoints.

9

Types of Tools - Flowcharts and Maps

We've talked about the servicescape and creating a journey map of the patient's physical experience. These are great tools for us to use as we work to craft an emotional experience for the patient. However, they fall short as we work to improve the process because they leave out many steps, especially the back-office steps.

In this chapter, we will look at tools that help identify the current state of our process and help us improve it. One of the tools we should use is a flowchart. A flowchart is a graphical representation of the work being performed—who does it, when it is done, and what that process looks like as we deliver the care.

A lot of folks will use the workflow map we create. It is nothing more than a visual representation of a process. It provides you something you can wrap your head around and understand. Once you know it, you can then improve it.

We will use maps to determine the current state of our process. It will help us answer questions such as, "Are the processes occurring the way they should?" These maps will provide a starting point for the improvement of a process, and they give us the ability to identify the roles and responsibilities of the process. Finally, they give us the ability to maintain the process once we've implemented the change.

Types of Flowcharts

There are three basic types of flowcharts we will use as we set out to improve any process. The first type of flowchart we will use is a **high-level flowchart**. This is a brief overview of the process being studied. Next, a **detailed flowchart** is going to lay out every step of the process. It's going to include decision points, waiting times, and feedback loops. The third type of flowchart you will use is a **swim lane chart**. A swim lane is a detailed map, but then it breaks out each process, or steps in that process, carried out by the different roles of the individuals across the multiple stages of the process.

To add confusion to the mix, these tools are often referred to as flowcharts, flow maps, flow diagrams, flow sheets, and process maps. They're all the same thing. It doesn't matter what you call them. What matters is that you create a visual representation of a process, a diagram of the sequence of events in a process from start to finish.

Why We Should Use Charts

A picture is worth a thousand words. A flowchart can save you a thousand minutes. These charts provide our staff (and us) with a visual representation of the process we're involved with. They allow us to determine if things are happening the way we think they are or should be.

Drafting our first chart is the starting point for the improvement of any process. We cannot make real, sustainable progress if we don't know where we are starting. We will use these charts to help us understand the current state of our process.

As we craft our charts, they will allow us to identify the roles and responsibilities of the process. It helps us determine who is doing what, when, and why in a process. Sometimes we might need to shift the who or what or when around. Using these charts will help us assign roles and responsibilities.

Finally, these charts will help us maintain the process once it is optimized. When we hire new people, they will need to know what the processes are. Using these charts will help them get up to speed quickly and understand how they fit into the organization's work. They will also provide guidance should questions arise as they work through the process. Referring to a chart will help answer many of their questions and save yourself time.

Levels of Flowcharts

As noted earlier, there are three basic types: high-level, detailed, and swim lane charts. Each type of chart will contain as much or as little information as necessary depending upon the needs of the organization and those who will be using the charts.

There are four levels of information when using flowcharts. The first level is the high-level; in layman's terms, the 30,000-foot view of the process. This is the simplest and contains enough information to understand the basic steps of the process. The second level is more detailed in information and becomes granular in the details of the steps. The third level is a swim lane chart, and it outlines duties, responsibilities, and hand-offs in the process. The fourth level is the most comprehensive and details steps down to the keystroke, button pushed, etc. These are the basis of a standard operating procedure.

My Examples

I will use the processes used by staff in the recovery room. This might be any recovery room in the US. (Fig. 9.1)

Fig. 9.1

This here would be an example of a high-level process in terms of a recovery room. A patient arrives in PACU and is handed over to the carer—the recovery room nurse. Assess the vitals, treat as needed, identify the next appropriate unit, provide a report to that unit, and then transfer the patient to the next unit. That would be an example of a high-level process. This is usually the first chart we will make. We begin by outlining the big things, the big steps, on the canvas. We're using broad brush-strokes with this chart. After we have developed this chart, we can dive into the process and get into the finer granular details.

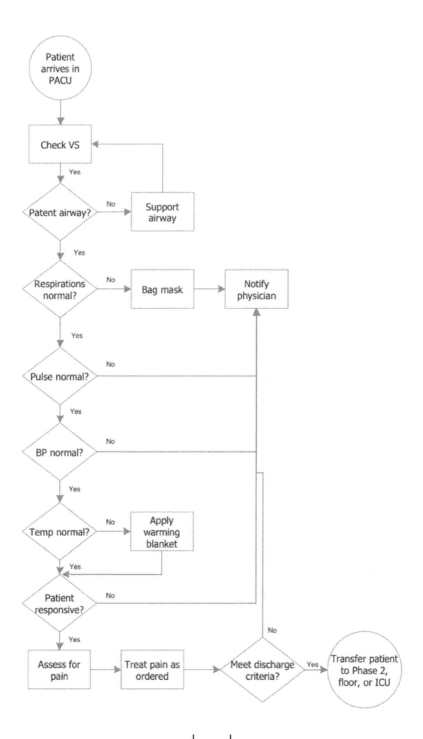

A detailed map would look something like this (Fig. 9.2). The patient arrives in PACU, and the nurse checks the vital signs. Does the patient have a patent airway? Yes, she doesn't need to support the airway and check the vitals again. Are the respirations normal? No. Bag mask the patient and notify the physician. Or, there are respirations, and she proceeds to the next action point.

We've all seen processes like this. If you look at any Advanced Cardiac Life Support algorithm, they are nothing more than a bunch of different processes in an algorithm. What we are attempting to do as we create these charts is to gain an understanding of the necessary steps, the proper order of those steps, and identify the decision points along the way. These charts will also help those involved in the process with their decision-making later.

After we develop our detailed process map, the next chart that is helpful is a swim lane chart. With a swim lane chart, we are going to take the detailed map we created and break it out into the roles of the individuals who are involved in that process.

So let's say a CRNA or resident delivers a patient to the recovery room. Not only do they physically move the patient to a different environment, but they also transfer knowledge and information about the patient to someone else involved in the process. Once they've given a report to the recovery room nurse, the nurse will run through the algorithm of recovering a patient from anesthesia. You will notice there are a few times where the nurse will be required to notify the physician, who then prescribes a treatment as indicated by the information provided by the nurse and observed with the patient. The physician provides instructions to the nurse, who carries out those orders. After that, the nurse then goes back through the algorithm.

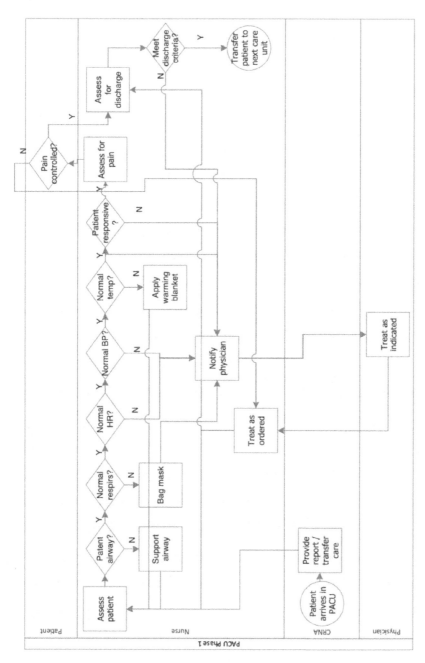

Fig 9.3

Of note, there are a few points in the process where the patient becomes involved in their own care. This is something we frequently overlook in healthcare. It's important to point out that the patient also has a role and responsibilities in our processes. They will be an active participant in the care we provide. For example, is their pain controlled? Yes or no? Their participation is required if the process is to address their comfort level fully.

Eventually, the process terminates (reaches its endpoint) when the patient is transferred to another unit, such as the ICU, the floor, or to phase two recovery. The transfer is a separate process with its own steps, roles, and responsibilities.

The swim lane chart (Fig. 9.3) will help us begin to see whose roles are in the process and what role they play. This can be helpful in terms of figuring out what roles, clearly defining roles and responsibilities in the process, as well as identifying points where you might have hand-off issues, and data can be missed. A swim lane is very helpful for identifying that as well.

You've been introduced to a couple of different ways to analyze a process with a high-level, a detailed level, and then a swim lane. These tools will help you as you begin to map out and understand the process. After you understand the current state of your process, you can then design and implement your improvements. In the next chapter, we will walk through the steps of crafting these maps.

Takeaways

> ➤ Flowcharts will be critical as you work to identify a process and improve it.
> ➤ Begin with the big picture and work down to fine details.
> ➤ Use swim lanes to help understand each person's role and their responsibilities in the process.

10 | Creating Service Maps

Imagine attempting to drive across the country from New York to Seattle or San Francisco without a map. How easy would it be? How long do you think it would take? How efficient do you think you might be? It would be challenging to make the road trip without a map. It can be done, but will likely involve a few detours, wrong turns, and wasted fuel and time. But with a map, we can plan how we'll get from the East Coast across the fruited plain to the West Coast. If we wouldn't think about making a road trip without a map, why would we attempt to improve a process without a plan? It might seem silly or perhaps a time-intensive low yield effort, but it will pay dividends.

The Map Legend

When I started flying many years ago, I had to learn how to read an entirely new type of map. Different colors, symbols, and numbers all have meaning on an aeronautical map. The one thing that helped me quickly learn what those symbols mean was the legend on the front lower corner of the map. As we begin to create our map, we should learn what the various symbols represent. This will helps us as we create the map.

Circles or ovals are used at the beginning and endpoints of our process. Squares or rectangles represent the activity to be done at that step in the process. Diamonds represent decisions that must be made in the process. When I create maps, these are the three main symbols I use. For completeness and for those who want detailed maps, I've included other symbols in figure 10.1.

The First Steps

The good news is we can make our service maps as simple or complex as we want. Sometimes simple maps work best. Other times, a complex, detailed map is required to solve the problem. Our maps will serve as a diagnostic tool, much like our stethoscopes. But first, before we begin using any tool, a good physician begins by asking questions. The first question should be, "What is the process we are attempting to outline?" Don't take this step lightly. Make it too broad, and you'll find yourself in the weeds quickly.

At the top of our piece of paper, whiteboard, or our preferred device, we will write the answer to that question. It might be **Patient Flow Through Clinic** or **Pre-operative Assessment**. Underneath that, we will write the date we create this map and what we think it's supposed to do. Off to the side somewhere, write down those individuals who are providing input as we craft the map. This step will help you identify the roles and responsibilities of the people in the process, as well as make sure you've consulted with the people you need to.

The next step is to define the starting point and endpoint. This is important because we want to keep scope creep to a minimum and help us identify the work we are examining. On the left side, we will write the starting point, and on the right, we will write the endpoint.

Now that we have identified these points, the purpose of the process, and some folks who are potentially involved, we can begin to map out the process. We start by asking a few questions.

Start With Questions

The next step is asking questions to help guide us as we build our map. Here are a few questions to help you get started as you begin to diagram your process.

> Does this process support the mission and purpose of the business?" Remember, the mission and purpose of the organization is the **what** and the **why** of the business. **What** is the service you provide, and the **why** is the benefit or reason for the patient. If a process doesn't support the mission and purpose, serious thought should be given as to the reasons why the process exists.

> Does each activity add value? Some processes might not add value to the organization. If they don't, then eliminate the process. Sometimes the value might be difficult to see, particularly those processes in the back-office or areas with low patient contact. They might still be necessary and add value, though. The purpose of this question is to help us define that value.

> Who is responsible for this process? Who owns this process? Since the organization is composed of people, some person is responsible for the process. The responsibility of the process typically falls upon those people who are involved in the process. A good leadership tip is for you to push the responsibility and decision-making of a process as low as possible. This empowers those people who are doing the work to take ownership and responsibility for the process.

> Is the process in control? What is the error rate of the process? How many mistakes are being made in the process? Are those mistakes a function of the process or the people in the process? Answers to these questions might be hard to hear but will give you insight into whether you have a people or process problem. Usually, I start my improvement initiatives with the assumption the process

is faulty and needs to be fixed. However, there are times when after studying a process, it's a particular individual who needs to be replaced in the process.

➤ Is it efficient? Are there any delays in the process? If so, why and when? Can these delays be avoided or shortened? How much time elapses from the beginning to the end of the process? How much money is spent as a result of the process? These questions will help you define not only the financial cost of the process but the personnel and time cost too.

➤ Can it be improved? Is the process as good as it will get at this time? If you have determined the process cannot get any better in terms of cost, efficiency, or time, then document that point. Make a note to revisit the process in a year or so to verify your initial findings. Sometimes things are as good as they can get. Your job then is to ensure they stay that way and do not worsen.

➤ Is it possible to develop a standard for this process? If this process is good, then perhaps you can use it as the standard and then push that standard out across your organization.

➤ Does this need to be moved up or back in the timeline in order to improve the efficiency and effectiveness of the process? Sometimes you will discover you can make a process more efficient if you take a step to an earlier point in the process. If this process is a part of a larger process, such as pre-operative evaluation of a patient before their surgery, moving certain activities to an earlier point can save time, energy, and money. For example, if we have a patient scheduled for elective surgery but they have a few co-morbid diseases such as coronary artery disease, diabetes, and sleep apnea, getting that patient evaluated earlier is better than waiting until the day before the scheduled procedure.

> ➢ Who is involved in the process? We will want to identify those individuals. This is going to take a team effort. You will want to do this for a variety of reasons. First, by identifying all parties involved in the process, you can ensure you have a complete understanding of it. Second, you can pick a champion or two to help as we develop and implement change. Third, we will have resources as we gather facts, data, and material. Fourth, we can have others help us craft the process by soliciting those members in the process.

It's a Team Process

Building your process map should be a team process. Gather everybody in a room and focus on developing the diagrams of your process. Lock the door, turn off the phones, and spend some time **together** developing these maps with the team. Start simple. Craft the overall map first and then create a detailed map. After you've identified the roles and responsibilities, we can create a swim lane map to help us understand our process.

Once you've created your process maps, we will want to verify they are correct. We may validate the map by walking through it with the team. Are the maps a true representation of the process as it currently exists? After you've mapped the process, ask, "Does this process support our mission and purpose?"

Finally, it's important to recognize that change won't affect nor benefit all of the stakeholders in the same manner. Some changes might benefit one stakeholder while adding work to another. Stay focused on the mission and purpose of the organization and the process as you work through change. Remember, there are no possessive pronouns in the mission and purpose—it's focused on the benefits to the patient.

Things to Consider as We Analyze the Maps

As we begin to analyze the map after you've designed it, some questions you're going to want to ask are:

> ➤ Where are the bottlenecks? Where are queues forming in the process? What might be causing delays in the service we provide? Every process will have a bottleneck. Just like any reaction we learned about in biochemistry, a rate-limiting step will exist. The first step in dealing with a bottleneck is to identify it. We will learn more about dealing with queues in a later chapter.

> ➤ How much rework and time wasted is being required? Why is rework occurring? Where are the errors occurring in the process? Is it a problem with the process or the people involved in carrying out the process? Begin with the idea that the process is in error. If you discover it's not the process, but the people, then you can deal with personnel professionally and objectively.

> ➤ Where might there be role ambiguity? Are there any steps that are duplicated? Are there any unnecessary steps, and where are the handoffs at work? Handoffs are critical points in the process where errors can creep into the work being done. These are areas where there is a risk in terms of quality and safety. Take extra time when a handoff point has been identified and understand how the information is being passed along the process. Omission and additions to the information are likely the sources of error.

A Way to Prime the Creative Pump of the Team

As we begin to set about improving processes with our team, it might be worth spending a little time warming up together. A simple exercise can help the team blend together as well as teach the fundamentals of process improvement. To get our team going, we can start with a simple exercise such as diagramming how to make a cup of coffee.

The first step is to obtain agreement among the members about the starting and endpoints—next, a list of the materials needed to make a cup of coffee. For the purposes of the exercise, use a pot of coffee rather than the simple single-cup machines. The elements needed are the coffee machine, pot, energy source (unless you're outside at a campfire), water, and coffee beans or grounds. If beans are used, then a way to grind the beans might be needed. After the list of the required equipment has been made, set about by diagraming the process.

We can begin with a simple, high-level map if needed, but with a simple task such as this, we can dive into a detailed map. Maybe we assign a few roles and craft a swim lane too. Who's responsible for obtaining the coffee? Where is it kept? What type of water is being used? Bottled or tap? If bottled water, who is responsible for getting it?

The important lesson of the exercise is to get the team on the same page and help them learn how to map a process on a simple harmless process. Once they've warmed up to the idea and have a little exercise, the experience and results we obtain dealing with the real processes will be better.

During the exercise, it's important to ask the team, "What did everyone discover? Does everyone understand what a process map is and what the importance of a process map is? Did the team work together to determine the start and endpoints?" We will get a good idea of how well the team will function together. Did the team have disagreements about anything, and how were those disagreements handled? How might those be better handled in the future? Finally, and perhaps most importantly, did everyone participate in the exercise? If some people didn't participate, why not? If they are not going to participate in making a cup of coffee, they may not participate in improving a larger process. When we're working to improve a process, we want everybody to participate.

Building a Swim Lane Map

Keep in mind that less is more when starting any improvement initiative. The goal is to use the bare minimum effort for a balance between functionality and clarity.

Identify the Roles

Who is responsible for what? Why are they responsible? What are their duties? Identifying these roles will help us ensure we have included the right people. They will give us guidance and input as to what is and isn't working in the process.

Where are the handoffs? Things typically go wrong during the handoff of work. Typically data is omitted or altered innocently. Remember the telephone game from grade school or a leadership workshop? Humans have a hard time remembering things.

What is the function of the job? What is the actual work being performed? What are the tasks? What is required for the tasks to be completed properly and on time?

Who has the most at stake? Who understands the end-to-end flow the best? Who has the authority to make the necessary changes in the process? We want to define who owns the process. They should be involved in the discussions of any improvement initiative.

Create the Canvas

At the top of the process name, we will write the name of the process. Below that, we will describe the desired process outcome. If we are creating a swim lane map, we will list the lanes for the roles of the individuals involved. Finally, we will take the detailed map and place the tasks in the appropriate lanes.

The Shapes

As noted earlier, keep it simple. Typically when I'm starting out, I use three shapes to illustrate a process: a circle, a square, and a diamond. As I dig into the process more, then I'll add additional shapes to represent the various activities.

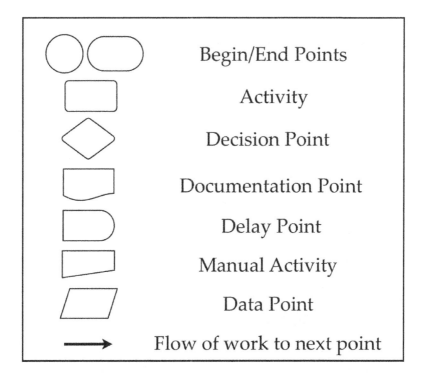

Begin/End Points

Activity

Decision Point

Documentation Point

Delay Point

Manual Activity

Data Point

Flow of work to next point

The How

In a service process, people are using physical and knowledge resources to create a service that is beneficial to the patient. Therefore, we should list the resources necessary for each activity and task in our process. Make a note of the quantity, where the resources are kept, how long they last, and the like. Along the way, you might find some tasks actually require multiple steps to complete. How detailed you get is up to you and your team.

After the Map Is Made

Once the map has been created, validated, and an improvement plan has been crafted, it's important that you use it. Once we have invested the time and energy in the exercise, we have to use the process map.

Process improvement isn't interviewing only a handful of people, if any at all. We don't want to map the process that we wish rather than the one we have. We begin by making the one that we have. It's good to know what you want in the future, but you need to know what your current state is. We don't want to ignore the opinions of those who know the process best. Most importantly, we don't put the map on a shelf or in a drawer and never look at it again. So if we're going to spend the time and energy to create these maps, which are incredibly helpful when we go to improve our process, make sure we actually use these tools that we're learning about.

Takeaways

➢ Start with asking questions of everyone involved in the process.
➢ Use the maps to find bottlenecks, ambiguity, and other issues.
➢ Once the map is made, use it.

11 | Tips on Improving the Organization

Identify all the processes in your organization or area of responsibility and note how well they work, the number of complaints each has from both staff and patients, how long each one takes, and so on. Once the processes have been identified, rank them according to the amount of effort it will take to improve or implement the process versus the impact it's going to have upon the organization. It's likely some will have a high impact with low effort. These are easy or quick fixes. It could be argued we should begin with those processes.

Another option is to identify a process that is most critical to the organization and work on it first. This might be a high effort, high impact process. Depending upon the nature of the team and its dynamics, this might be a good starting point for an improvement initiative. If the team is new to each other, perhaps a smaller project should be addressed first.

There will be low processes that require a low effort to improve and have a low impact. It's recommended the processes be addressed after the high impact processes. Finally, there will be thankless tasks. These are those processes that have a high effort and low (or no) impact. Honestly, you're going to want to avoid those thankless tasks. If it's a high effort with low impact, we should question if it's worth the time and effort to fix them. Why waste time on those processes? It is a good exercise to identify those thankless tasks, so we know to avoid them. There's nothing worse than investing time, energy, and money in improving a process that yields low or no impact.

Go for the low-hanging fruit first. Try to spot ways where you can have some quick fixes and easy wins with the team early on. Sometimes those might not be available, and you'll have to roll up your sleeves and do some hard work.

Biases That Will Trip You Up

As we make plans to improve our processes, we can get tripped up with some biases either we or our people hold. We need to be aware of these biases so that we approach our improvement initiatives with a blank slate.

> ➤ **The Halo Effect**. This bias holds that if someone is good at one thing, then they are good at other things. Sometimes we hold this bias for others, and way too often, we hold it for ourselves. Just because we are smart and talented in one area doesn't necessarily make us good in other areas. This reminds me of training residents. Those residents who have good technical skills are deemed better sometimes or given more leeway than those who don't. What's curious is there are times when the skills don't match the fund of knowledge or ability to apply knowledge to the clinical situation. I know several physicians who think they are the smartest folks in the room, but when I watch them lead change, it doesn't go so well. I think personal halo effect bias is perhaps the biggest stumbling block we face.
> ➤ **Availability bias**. We see this bias quite a bit in medicine. "In my series of one or two, I've seen this. So, therefore, it must occur frequently." Just because it happens once or twice doesn't make it physical law. Be open to finding the root cause of the problem. Don't make assumptions.
> ➤ **Spurious awareness bias**. This is when we think we know things that really are not so. I saw this a bit with my kids when they were in elementary school. They talked as if they knew everything and were always right. I've even seen this

with a few colleagues. We must always be questioning our knowledge and understanding of the situation.

➢ **Anchoring bias.** People tend to latch onto information that is presented early in their discovery, and then fail to update the knowledge base when new information is presented. I think this is the reason we have continuing education requirements, so that we continually update our database and overcome our anchoring biases.

➢ **Recency bias.** We tend to pay more attention to what has happened recently, even if it's not representative of what usually happens. This is similar to our spurious awareness bias. We tend to remember the most recent events most clearly and make the assumption these are the standard.

➢ **Selective perception/confirmation bias.** We tend to give credence to what confirms our beliefs and discount those things that contradict our beliefs. We filter out those data points that do not support our underlying beliefs and assumptions, while quickly accepting those that do.

➢ **Memory/hindsight bias.** Most folks have a poor memory. We frequently remember things differently from what actually happened. This is one of the reasons we write notes in the medical chart, because our memory isn't always reliable.

Takeaways

➢ Ask yourself what biases are present as you work to improve your systems.

➢ Start with the easy wins, then work on the big projects.

➢ Focus on stuff that will make the biggest impact in either waste, safety, or costs.

12 | Managing the Process

In this chapter, we will examine how we manage the process. Let's begin by defining what the term *management* means. Management of a process involves two activities. The first is the measurement, or monitoring, of the process. The second is taking the appropriate corrective action when necessary. The first step is critical. If we get it wrong, then taking the proper corrective action is left to chance.

Management Defined

Measure

As we begin to manage our processes, the first task is to ensure we measure the right things. As we begin to pick our metrics, the most important question is, "Does your measurement support the mission and purpose? Does it support the process?" If the answer isn't a clear "yes", then spend some time rethinking the metric. After we pick the metrics, then we can manage the process and take action to control and improve the process.

What to Measure?

Picking the proper metrics can be easier if we ask the right questions. Some questions that will help you can clarity include:

➢ Is there a reason for the measurement?
➢ Can the results be acted upon?
➢ Does it measure what you want it to measure?
➢ Does it only measure what you want to measure?
➢ Is the measurement consistent?
➢ Are the results easy to interpret?
➢ Is it easily acted upon?
➢ What is the cost of the measurement?
➢ Is the information gained worth the cost?
➢ Will the measurement allow for or encourage undesirable behaviors?

When we measure something, we want to measure the right thing. In medicine, there are a lot of tests we can order and stuff we can monitor to determine the health of our patients. If we want to measure our diabetic patients' compliance over time, we could look at their blood glucose, but a hemoglobin A1C will give us a better understanding of how well they've done over time. One test only partially answers our question of control. The other will provide us with insight into the long-term trend.

When we monitor a process, we will apply the same thought process. We want to measure the right thing with the right tool. We also want the measurement to support the mission and purpose of our organization. Does the measurement support the process? If so, then we can use it to manage the process and take action to control and improve the measurement. That is the definition of managing any process. The question with any metrics should always be, "Are we managing—are we monitoring—the right thing, and are we able to effect change and improve the data obtained?"

So what do we want to measure? A better question might be, is there a reason or justification for the measurement? Nothing comes without a cost. Sometimes costs are apparent, and sometimes they are hidden. Any measurement we make will come with a cost. What are those costs of the measurement?

Another critical question is, can the results of the measurement be acted upon? If we cannot take action to influence the measurement, do we need to measure it? Why spend time and energy on something we cannot influence? I will agree that sometimes it is necessary, but I would argue we should focus on those things we *can* control.

Does the measurement measure what we want it to measure? What is the scope of the measurement? How specific and sensitive is it? Does it measure only what we want to measure, or does it measure too much? Is the measurement consistent and repeatable? Are the results easy to interpret?

Finally, will this measurement allow for or encourage undesirable behaviors? Earlier I mentioned that measurements have costs—some direct and obvious, and others not so much. Sometimes what we measure can have unintended consequences and encourage our people to act in ways that are contrary to the organization. We must make sure our measurements and any rewards are aligned. I can remember my flight was ten minutes behind schedule, and when I walked to the gate of my connection, the gate was closed. However, they sat there for another fifteen minutes before they pushed back. The FAA measures on-time from when the front door is closed, not when they take off. The airline, in an attempt to look good in the eyes of the FAA and thus the public, closes their doors to hit a metric. As a customer, I was not happy, and now I don't fly with them anymore. We have countless stories in sales and middle management where individuals have acted in their own best interest and contrary to what is best for the organization because of a metric that was in place. Always ask if the parameter we've chosen will entice someone to act in a way that doesn't benefit the organization.

What Needs to Be Measured

So what must be measured? There are a few drivers of success. The first one is developmental and operational measurements, and external and financial measurements. Developmental measurements are things like staff turnover, staff satisfaction, employee engagement, service innovation—these measurements are focused on how we develop our people in the organization.

Operational measurements examine outcomes of the process, such as wait times, patients per day, complaints that we receive. External measurements investigate outcomes of the process and might include items such as customer satisfaction, number of repeat patients, number of referrals we have. Finally, financial measurements would be our total costs, our cost per patient, revenue per patient, and budget variance. Just like the four Ps of exemplary patient care, we need to watch our people, productivity, performance, and profitability.

I suggest picking a couple of different measurements from each of the four categories—people, productivity, performance, and profitability. Also, as stated earlier, pick ones that link the measurements to our mission and purpose. Make sure the metrics support, reinforce, and communicate our objectives and goals. Pick metrics that people focus on, and drive change. Ask if there are any investments and actions associated with the metric.

It's important to monitor internal data, such as financial and operational metrics. However, the key metric that we all should watch is patient satisfaction. Internal metrics are wonderful and necessary, but those do not tell us how the patient feels and experiences our services. We have no idea what emotions the patient is experiencing unless we ask them. This is an important point—if you're not doing patient satisfaction surveys, you're missing a critical piece of the puzzle. We might think we're doing great because we have all this other great stuff, our staff's engaged, wait times are down, our revenues are up—but we don't really understand why until we add that last piece. That piece is how the patient feels about this experience that you provide them.

Obtaining Patient Feedback

There are a couple of different ways we can get this important data. We can use questionnaires, surveys, and even the experiences of a mystery patient. We might add a complaint and compliment analysis. When something happens, or we aren't getting the results we desire, we might have to perform a root cause analysis.

When we're developing and designing sampling tools or surveys, avoid changing the questions of the survey. As we change the questions, we lose the ability to track and trend the results over time. Also, don't ask too many questions. Longer questionnaires usually have poor participation, or people may just say, "I'm tired of answering these questions. I'm done." Don't send too many surveys. If we notice a trend of bad or undesired answers to our surveys and don't make changes, our patients may stop filling them out. Remember, we asked the patient to complete a survey. They invested energy and time into answering our questions. We should honor that investment by addressing the issues revealed in the results.

There are a few issues when we use customer satisfaction tools. The first is these tools can use a lot of resources to collect and analyze the data. Someone has to send the survey and input the data. If the data is via a paper survey, we will need to pay someone to input the data. There is also the cost of analyzing the data. Do we have the software and resources to crunch the numbers? Second, sometimes the data isn't used to make an impact. It's important to keep in mind satisfaction doesn't always mean success. Finally, the data is always at risk of being manipulated to tell a story a different way. As Mark Twain said, "There are lies, damn lies, and statistics."

When we are looking at our metrics, we want to set up targets or benchmarks that provide us with valuable data points. We will want to compare them from month to month, week to week, quarter to quarter. We want to spot a change as soon as possible.

Just be careful and mindful of the metrics you pick when you are beginning to monitor and make improvements. Make certain that they support the mission and purpose, and the cost of the data is worth what it is when you go to use that data.

In the next chapter, we will discuss how to lead our people involved in the process. We will examine what stresses they might deal with and how, as leaders, we can help them make changes and take responsibility for the process.

Takeaways

➤ Managing a process involves measuring and taking the proper corrective action.
➤ Picking the proper metrics is key to keeping a process in control.
➤ Solicit patient feedback frequently.

13

Leading People

In the previous chapter, we discussed how to manage the process. Although that is important, what's more critical is leading the people in the process. I believe we manage operations, but we always lead people.

Stressors

Our people will feel stressors from two sides: the organization and the patient. As we lead them, we must be aware of the stresses we might induce in them. Some of the **company stressors** are the process itself, the availability of resources required for the process, the metrics we use to monitor the process and their performance, and the feedback we provide them and how we give it.

They also feel stress from the patients. **Patient stressors** include their expectations, their attitudes, the personal risk our people experience as a result of the care, and their ability to comply with the demands and needs of the patient.

Remember the four Ps of exemplary patient care? Our people are the ones that do the work. Sometimes, depending on the organization, our people can be stuck in the middle between the needs of the clinic and those of the patient. Sometimes they will feel stressed because they are pulled in two different directions, such as ordering an expensive test or prescribing a costly drug.

Leading our people will help prevent them from feeling as if they are stuck in the middle and must choose between the two perspectives. How will they feel being stuck in the middle if the organization has a valid mission and purpose? Honestly, I don't believe they will. Our people will feel pulled in different directions when the organization doesn't have a valid mission and purpose, that mission and purpose isn't embedded into the culture of the organization, or we have created metrics by which we judge their performance that does not align with the mission and purpose. That is how our people can become stressed.

Imagine a nursing manager who knows she should bring an extra nurse in for an upcoming shift, but because she has to face financial metrics, they opt not to, knowing it might cause extra work for their nurses who will work the shift. That manager is pulled in two directions. If she thinks they should bring in the extra nurse, then she is doing so because she knows the patients and other staff will benefit. But when financial metrics are placed at the top of the list, then that is the guiding light for her decision.

However, if metrics related to patient care and satisfaction are used, then a different choice is made. This is why we must create the right metrics when monitoring any process. How much risk does a hospital face when the staff is stressed? What happens to their response times to their patients? How might their attitudes change under these conditions? As leaders, we must be aware of our people's emotions and attitudes.

What happens if we don't address their emotions and attitudes when we attempt to improve a process? How successful do you think it will be? It's been my experience that people who feel listened to, cared for, and led by competent leaders implement change must faster and more permanently than those who don't.

As we begin to design the process and implement change, we must keep in mind what stressors our people will face. What are the stressors from our side—that of the organization—and ourselves as leaders? What expectations do they have about us, our leadership, and the changes we want to implement? What stressors might arise from the patients as we change things? Our people will feel those too. Never forget that.

Issues Your People Face

Our people will face many issues as they perform the services for our patients. Sometimes they will have issues with motivation to do the work and deal with patients. Other times, they may face a mismatch with their abilities and the role they play. Or perhaps we haven't done a good job defining their role and duties. What is their relationship like with us, their leaders? Their superiors? Their coworkers? Their patients?

Your people can face a few different issues. They're going to have motivational issues. They may not fully understand what their role is or how they fit. They may have issues with relationships with coworkers, their superiors, or even patients. They can be at risk depending on the environment and experience stress. We're all well aware of what stress and risk can do to the level of a service provided.

Patient-Centric Issues

There are many patient-centric issues our people will face as they deliver care. First, there is the constant, never-ending presence of patients in high-contact services such as RNs in the ER, admissions, our office staff. Burnout is a possibility because of the constant intensity of the area.

Second, how providers view the care they deliver sometimes is different from the perceptions of the patient. Patients like to think the service they receive is special; that they are special. While that is true, occasionally, providers might feel differently, and they might not know it. The procedures they perform are routine for them. That "routine-ness" can be a source of stress for our people and our patients. If you've ever heard someone call an OR desk describing their add-on as a procedure rather than a patient, then you know what I'm referring to.

Third, the expectations of the patients are frequently a source of stress for our people. Our patients might expect the same level of service they received from someone else somewhere else. This could be good or bad for you, but keep in mind—we are always being compared to something else, some other experience. Some patients may have completely unrealistic expectations of our staff, our service, and our capabilities. When they voice these unrealistic expectations, stress will arise in our people. Finally, the mood of the customer impacts the service providers. If they are angry, sad, in pain, these emotions will affect and stress our people. We all have encountered those individuals who are less than pleasant, and we have to be on guard to make certain that their attitude doesn't affect us and the service we provide.

How You Can Help Your People

As a leader, you must help your people. Provide them leadership. We should be a good role model. Build and use teams effectively to share not only the burden but the wealth. As a leader, we also need to ensure the roles and duties are clearly understood by the members of the team.

Sometimes our people may be helped if we provide them scripts and training to standardize patient encounters. We may also build into the process of their decision-making abilities. Define and allow for appropriate levels of their description. Doing so will empower them and place responsibility for the process on their shoulders. They will become more engaged and accountable. If done properly, they will become more independent and even initiate improvement initiatives on their own.

Helping your team members achieve their personal short and long-term goals will aid in developing a culture of continuous improvement. Begin by focusing on their goals that align with the mission and purpose of the organization. Look for training opportunities and development in the skill sets that will benefit them, the organization, and the patient. Maintaining a motivated team member will help them stay engaged in continuous improvement and deliver exemplary patient care.

Four Things to Manage as a Leader

As we lead our team, there are a few items we will need to manage if we are to be effective. If we consistently focus on these things, we will be able to drive the change in our organization.

> **Their attention.** We must be able to capture their hearts and minds through effective communication. Our messages must be clear and concise. They should also be mission and purpose-driven.

> **The bigger picture.** This is where a valid mission and purpose statement shows its strength. Our mission must be at the forefront, acting as a guiding light. Doing this will aid us in staying focused on broader issues. During an improvement initiative, it's easy to get focused on the little stuff to the detriment of the bigger issues. Take care not to focus on the process so much you lose sight of the mission and purpose.

> **Their trust.** As leaders, we must be reliable. We demonstrate this by being a good role model, being clear and consistent in our communication. Trust is challenging to earn and very easy to lose. Without their trust, our improvements will take longer because they won't commit everything to it.

> **Yourself.** We must know our strengths and weaknesses. Recognize we don't always have all the answers. Be willing to listen and receive information from our people with a blank slate. Approach the issues we face with a growth mindset.

Now that we've addressed issues leading our people in the process, we should deal with a source of stress for our people— the available resources. In the next chapter, we will examine strategies to manage our resources in a process.

Takeaways

> ➢ Recognize there are stressors your people will experience.
> ➢ Work to manage their attention, their trust, the bigger picture, and yourself.
> ➢ Understanding the stressors your people face will enable you to effectively lead them.

14

Managing Resources

So far, we learned how to map a process, pick metrics that work for monitoring the process, and how to lead our people. The next step is to ensure the proper management of the resources available for the service. In this chapter, we will examine a variety of tools we can use to plan for the best use of our resources. We will begin our discussion by examining an important limitation of any service—capacity.

Capacity

We must realize all services have a specific capacity. We can only do so much in a certain period of time with the resources and people we have available to us. When we are trying to determine capacity, we need to ask if we have sufficient resources to deal with the anticipated demand. And not only that but do we also have the resources to meet the quality of service cost-effectively?

In some clinical settings, capacity can be quite challenging to deal with, particularly when we have variable demand and offer a wide array of services. Any tertiary referral center deals with this issue daily. If we have several different practitioners who are providing different service lines, it can be very challenging to determine what our true capacity is and how actually to use that capacity appropriately.

It becomes a balancing act between being underutilized and being overutilized. The first one costs us money, and the other drives our people nuts and creates stress in the workplace. Our capacity then becomes a balancing act.

Determine Your Capacity

As you might have noticed in this book, I like to ask questions. The first one I would ask is: Do we have sufficient resources to deal with the anticipated demand? Then, are we able to meet the quality of service needed cost-effectively?

Do we know what exactly we need to provide the service in a quality manner? This is why we map the process in the beginning—to help us understand what is required to provide this particular service.

What is the maximum level of activity over a period of time a process can *consistently* achieve under *normal operating conditions* and still *add value* to the patient? Any number of metrics might help us determine this value. It could be the number of patients seen in a day in the clinic. Or perhaps the number of surgeries performed in a day. Be careful you don't define your capacity at a high level where the patient feels the level of service declines. For example, if we know we cannot perform eight surgeries in one day, then we shouldn't schedule eight surgeries in one day. What's worse for our patient satisfaction, waiting a week and having an elective surgery done during the day, or making the patient wait all day and undergoing the elective surgery late in the evening? One's better for the surgeon, perhaps, but what's best for the patient? We should be careful not to define our capacity at a high level where the patient feels that the level of service will actually decline because we're so constrained.

Measuring Capacity

Measuring our capacity can be complicated with multiple variables. Our case mix, or complexity of the patients, is one thing that can affect our capacity. Four-hour back surgeries or patients with a problem two pages long will take longer to see. Having a bunch of those on the schedule will affect our capacity in terms of the required time needed per patient.

Aside from time restraints, there are resource constraints. Perhaps we only have one or two exam rooms or only one cystoscopy pan, or only one surgical team. The resources we have will limit our capacity. Once we have identified our time, resource, and personnel constraints, we can begin to plan our capacity.

Plan the Capacity

Once we have identified our capacity, it is time to plan for it. There are two broad planning approaches we should consider—long-term and short-term planning. Long-term planning involves the locations, the capabilities of the site, and the flexibility and how we're planning to do that. Our day-to-day issues are more short-term issues. We can plan for the short-term by using either a level, a chase, or a demand planning strategy.

Level Planning

With a level planning approach of capacity, we maintain our expensive resources at a constant level. This will require us to deal with the consequences of patient satisfaction and the occasional quality issue, but the goal is to maximize the utilization of the expensive resources, whether that's the physical resources or our people's availability.

We see this approach often with the airlines. They plan on no-shows and overbook the flight. We might consider doing the same in our practice. The most valuable resource might be our time, so, therefore we want to schedule as many patients as possible during the day. No-shows and downtime hurt our bottom line. This approach, although it helps preserve the value of the resources, can have adverse effects on patient satisfaction.

You plan on no-shows, and you overbook, just like airlines plan on no-shows, and they overbook. So let's say you schedule four patients for 2:00 pm. Patients will arrive in batches. Customer satisfaction may suffer because of the inconsistent levels of service, and you're just planning that one patient will be a no-show. So you only have three patients booked at 2:00, and one will be seen at 2:00, one will be seen at 2:10 or 2:15, and the third at 2:20 or 2:30. However, the danger is that they think their appointment is for 2:00.

Just like overbooking a flight, we can overbook an hour. Perhaps we schedule four patients at 2:00 pm and have all the patients arrive at the same time. Obviously, someone will be waiting longer than the others. This wait might negatively impact their experience. However, if we have a no-show, we aren't hurt as much. Taking this approach might also lead to inconsistent levels of service to our patients, depending on how our gamble has paid off. We're better if we have two no-shows vs. no no-shows. There is a danger in this approach in that we might become complacent and fail to make attempts to cut or reduce the emotional cost of the waiting patient.

Our queue management systems are another useful tool to manage and plan for level demand. We must be careful of the message we send to our patients. Queues can sometimes say, "Your time is worthless." Furthermore, patients may only wait for as long as their time is worth. So if it's going to take twenty minutes to get a McDonald's cheeseburger, they're probably not going to wait. But if it's major hip surgery or something else, they may wait that long. But it is a balancing act, and you have to realize that the patient is investing their time, and they will measure the value of their time they've spent waiting for you compared to the value of the service that you will provide. If they perceive their time waiting as more valuable than the service we provide, they might leave. We will go more in-depth in bottlenecks and queues in the next chapter.

Chase

The second option available to us is to chase the demand. With this model, we are attempting to match our supply to the demand as much as possible by building flexibility into the operation. Our prime objective with this approach is to maintain a high level of service. We want to be available for a fast response in the most efficient manner possible.

Our staff's availability to work will go up and down with demand during the day. We bring more people in to do the work during peak times and send them home during off-peak times. When I was in college, I worked as a phlebotomist, and my shift was a few hours in the early morning during peak times. They had three of us come in for those peak times. It worked well for them. Perhaps we should consider that as an option for our patients. Bring in more resources during our peak times, such as over the noon hour.

Demand

With this approach, we attempt to create demand for our services through marketing and other tools. We might want to try pricing strategies. For instance, we might promote off-peak demands. If it's possible, we might offer incentives for patients to visit during our non-peak times. We might not be able to offer financial incentives to the patients, but we can offer other perks to encourage them to move their appointments to off-peak times. We might also restrict service at peak times. Finally, in the demand model, rather than chasing or changing capacity, try and influence the demand for your service, then kind of smooth the load out over the resources. There are also booking systems, which can give a patient an idea of what their wait time is.

Tips for Planning Your Work

There are many factors we want to consider when we are looking at our schedule. How and when we handle the work will vary. The first method we might think is a first-in-first-out; we take them in the order in which they were received. Another approach is to deal with the most valuable patient first. This method is fraught with ethical issues, but it might be worth considering in some situations. Finally, there is the critical work-first approach. We see this at work in the emergency room or critical care setting. We're going to take the most critical person first, and everybody else who is less critical will wait.

We might consider scheduling all our least intensive work first. The goal is to get the simple, easy stuff completed as quickly as possible, and save our most strenuous complex patients for later in the day. Or we may consider doing the opposite and dealing with the most complex patients first, and then schedule those routine follow-ups towards the later part of the day. Only you can decide what's best for you and your practice. The key is to give your schedulers very specific instructions in terms of when they can and cannot schedule certain types of patients. You will be granting them some control over your schedule, so you will want to involve them in the process.

In the next chapter, we will examine how we can help our patients cope with waiting. Queues and bottlenecks are unavoidable in a service process. However, we should do what we can to alleviate the wait.

Takeaways

> Create a clear flow of patients. Plan on who and when you'll be seeing certain types of patients.
> Ensure resources are available to meet the scheduled demand you've created.
> Create a schedule for interlinking activities. If you do minor procedures in the office, have a master schedule of the procedure room and the exam rooms. Also, plan out which staff will be in what areas throughout the day.

15

Bottlenecks

In the last chapter, we discussed how we might plan to manage the resources necessary for our process. In any process, whether it's manufacturing, a service process, or a chemical reaction, a bottleneck will exist. There is always a rate-limiting step. It's something common and inherent in the service industry, particularly when people are responsible for providing that service.

Bottlenecks are a part of the process, and they constrain or restrict the capacity of the process. The result of the constraint is a queue. How we manage our bottlenecks will have a massive impact on our patient satisfaction and overall efficiency of the service. The key to successfully dealing with a bottleneck is to identify and manage it.

Managing Bottlenecks

Once you've identified a bottleneck, devote more time, attention, energy, and resources to ensure maximum throughput is attained. Also, only move a bottleneck if absolutely necessary. Sometimes simply where a bottleneck exists in the process is enough in very complex systems and processes.

One approach to managing a bottleneck is the theory of restraints. To help minimize the effect of the bottleneck on the overall process, we must ensure only essential work passes through the bottleneck. If we eliminate all non-essential tasks from the bottleneck, we can ensure the bottleneck isn't dealing with unnecessary work. We don't want substandard work passing through the bottleneck. Redoing work can be costly in terms of time, energy, and money. Don't make the bottleneck worse by pushing incomplete, low quality work through it.

Sometimes there isn't anything we can do to eliminate the bottleneck. Simply knowing where it exists is enough in very complex systems. If we identify it, we can plan around it. It might have to stay where it is, and that's fine. However, we want to make sure that only the essential work passes through that bottleneck.

We must deal with the effects on our patients. What will our patients experience as they go through the bottleneck? Fortunately, there are a few rules of thumb we can use as we plan our servicescape and process. These are called the rules of time.

The Rules of Time

➢ **The perceived waiting time is greater than the actual waiting time.** We all do this. If the restaurant says it will be ten minutes for a table, at about five minutes, I'm looking at my watch, wondering what's taking so long. That's when my wife reminds me it's only been five minutes. However, it feels so long to me. I'm sure you've experienced the same thing. Remember, the patients who are waiting on you will experience the same time warp.

➢ **Unoccupied time feels longer than occupied time.** If your patient is just waiting with nothing to do, the wait will seem longer compared to if they have something to occupy their time. Reading material, music, television, and even paperwork can be used to occupy their time as they wait. Think about ways you can occupy their minds and make their wait feel shorter.

➢ **Anxiety always makes the wait feel longer.** If your patient feels anxious about anything, the wait will feel longer to them. It's similar to the worry you might feel that you will miss a connecting flight. They are worried about what the report will be, what the diagnosis will be, whether they will get better. Have your staff do what they can to help them feel less anxious and demonstrate compassion as they wait.

➢ **Uncertain wait times feel longer than known or expected wait times.** Knowing is better than not knowing when you're waiting. When a patient checks in, have your staff give them an approximate wait time before they are called back. I personally experienced this a few years ago with my son. We checked into the physician's desk and waited and waited. After waiting for thirty minutes, I asked when we might be seen. Being a physician, I understand delays can happen. However, in this instance, the staff didn't know how long it would take nor what the reason was. Ultimately, we were taken back to the exam room about seventy-five minutes late. It was quite unusual for this physician, but I would have liked to know he got backed up and would be behind schedule. That seventy-five minutes felt like half a day. Your patients will experience the same feelings, and this has a dramatic impact on their satisfaction.

➢ **Unexplained wait times feel longer than explained wait times.** Had the physician's office told me the time and reason, I would have been more satisfied. Remember, always tell them the estimated wait time and the reason for the delay. Patients are more understanding than you might think. They also will take this action as a measure of good faith, honesty, and integrity.

➢ **Unfair wait times feel longer than equitable wait times.** We once visited a restaurant whose unwritten policy was to seat smaller parties before larger parties. So when a couple walked in after my party of three, we felt irritated, especially since they were seated at a small table with three chairs. Always be aware of the judgments your patients might make. Remember, the patient might overhear conversations your office staff might have with other patients. Those conversations, even though taken out of context, might lead to judgments of unfairness.

> **The greater the value of the service you are providing leads to the longer a patient will wait.** How long will you wait for a McDonald's cheeseburger? How long will you wait for a juicy, sizzling steak? A cup of broccoli compared to a wonderful salad? The value you place on the service or good you are about to receive determines your patience and how long you'll wait. Your patients will determine how long they have to wait to see you if you have patients complaining to you that they had to wait a long time, which says two things. First, they are dissatisfied. Second, it gives you insight into their perception of the value of the service you're providing them.

> **Waiting by yourself feels longer than when you're with someone.** Family and friends can be a real benefit to patients. They can provide physical and emotional support to your patients. They can also be a second set of ears that hear your instructions. They also can help the wait seem shorter. Consider encouraging loved ones, family, and friends to accompany your patient visits. It might just help your patients feel more satisfied.

> **Discomfort makes the wait feel longer than wait times when comfortable.** Whenever we hurt, time slows down. If you have patients in pain while they wait, do what you can to get them comfortable. This will demonstrate you care, are compassionate, and help them as they wait for you.

> **New patients will experience the wait longer than those established patients.** Patients who have never been to your practice will experience or perceive the wait longer than established patients. It's partly because they don't know what to expect. Established patients know what to expect and have, to an extent, accepted the waiting as

part of the process. New patients must learn your process and wait times. That's why keeping the patient informed, comfortable, and occupied can play a large role in a new patient's perceived experience of your practice.

As you deal with your wait times, remember to address the items above. Always keep them informed of the duration and reason for the wait. Make them comfortable and encourage them to bring along a loved one. Do what you can to occupy their time. Queues and waiting times are inevitable, but you can influence how the patient perceives the wait time and their satisfaction.

The Effect of Queues on Your People

Dealing with queues can also be stressful for our people. They know patients are waiting, sometimes in pain, and they want to help them. They also know the capacity is limited, yet they likely feel a duty to do their best. Be careful how we load our queues because everyone has a breaking point.

Our people will cope with the demand up to a point, and then they might *break*. When they *break*, they will either do so emotionally and treat the patient poorly, cut corners to reduce the queues and deliver lower-quality care, or simply become disengaged and sloppy.

Help your people deal with the queue. Be aware of the bottleneck—the stress placed upon your staff—and help them cope with the stress. We can help our people manage the queue and deal with the patients who are in the queue by giving them some strategies to do that. One way we can do that is to craft and distribute our service concept. That's our mission and purpose, and we should have it out where our people, as well as our patients, can see it.

Finally, we should do what we can to help our people develop coping strategies for when things become stressful.

When you're trying to help folks with things, like dealing with the stress of being in a queue, what does the customer-perceived quality or capacity look like? What measures or early signals tell you you're nearing the breaking point, or getting to the end of your rope? How might the patient suffer when you do reach that point? How will your employees suffer, and what can be done to reduce the impact on patients and employees, and what can be done to keep you from getting to the breaking point at all?

Factors to Consider When Creating Your Queues

There are three key aspects: the patient arrival rate, the rate at which patients can be seen, and the number of providers available. How fast are patients arriving at our clinic? How much time does it take to see a patient? How many providers are required to see a patient? What is the demand, and do we have the resources to meet that demand?

Questions to Ask When Dealing With a Bottleneck

To help you identify and deal with your bottlenecks, start by asking the following questions. They will provide you insight into the impact of the bottleneck on your patients and your people.

- ➤ What does the customer quality look like? How does the customer feel? How do they perceive the capacity of the clinic?
- ➤ What metrics or early signals tell you when you're nearing the breaking point?
- ➤ How does the patient suffer when the breaking point is reached?
- ➤ How do your employees suffer?
- ➤ What can be done to reduce the impact on patients and staff?
- ➤ What steps can be taken to keep you from the breaking point?

Now that we've covered how to define your servicescape, map your process, manage the resources, lead your people, and deal with bottlenecks, it's time to discuss quality. In the next chapter, we will examine what quality is, how to define it, and how to monitor it.

Takeaways

> ➤ Identify the bottlenecks in your processes. Can they be eliminated or moved?
> ➤ Understand the effect of bottlenecks on your patients and how the rules of time affect them.
> ➤ Queues also add stress to your people. Do what you can to help your people cope with the stress of the bottleneck.

16 | Your Patient – Your Customer

As I went through my MBA classes, I was amazed by how my concept of the patient returned to that of prior to being a doctor for a few decades. In medical school, we are taught patients are important, but after time, we lose sight of their importance. In business school, one of my professors shared their definition of the customer.

- ➢ The customer is the most important person ever in this office, on the phone, or wherever we meet them.
- ➢ The customer is not dependent on us; we are dependent on them.
- ➢ The customer is not an interruption of our work; they are the purpose of it.
- ➢ We are not doing them a favor by serving them; they are doing us a favor by giving us the opportunity to do so.
- ➢ The customer is not someone to argue or match wits with. Nobody ever won an argument with a customer.
- ➢ The customer is a person who brings us their wants. It is our job to handle them profitably to them and to ourselves.

I think we as physicians recognize these apply to our patients. Our patients are our customers. Often, providers may be burned out, tired, and worn down. When they reach that point, they might lose sight of what a patient really is.

Tips on Retaining Customers

➢ Always, always, always say, "thank you."
➢ Reward their loyalty. Sometimes financial, sometimes with a caring follow-up. It might be a birthday card in addition to their annual exam reminder.
➢ Find a way to reward referrals. This is challenging but be creative.
➢ Solicit problems they face as they go through your process, and do what you can to fix them.

Why Customers Complain

Patients complain for a variety of reasons. They are almost always patient-centered. The complaint is a great way for you to gather information about your processes. Most patients don't complain for the sake of complaining. Often, they have real concerns or issues.

➢ They want a problem corrected. When they complain, ask questions that get to the root of the problem. They are voicing their concerns because they have a problem that hasn't been solved yet.

➢ They desire to help you prevent the problem from happening again to others. If one patient has an issue with your process, it is possible others are experiencing the same issue. Perhaps you have more patients that think the same thing, and they just aren't speaking up. It's similar to sitting in class, and someone asks a question. I guarantee others in the room had the same question, but only one person asked it. Taking this approach with complaints can help you improve your processes.

➢ They want an explanation of what occurred to them. When they complain, it might be because they don't under-stand what happened and why it happened. It's their way of requesting information and understanding. Try not to be defensive when receiving complaints because they might just be a cloaked method of requesting understanding on behalf of the patient.

➢   They want someone punished for what happened to them. Sometimes, they feel so insulted or accosted, and they want some to pay for their misery.

➢   They want money. Sometimes they might think the pain will improve with money. Asking good questions will help you get to the root problem and their real desire.

➢   They want to feel better. Sometimes simply voicing their complaints helps the patient feel better about the situation. It's therapy for them. Even though we might not be therapists, we can help the patients by simply being a soundboard. There is a fine line between allowing them to complain to get things off their chest and being a doormat. Never be a doormat. If they are abusive, don't tolerate it.

Tips on Dealing With Complaining Patients

Now that we understand the reasons patients complain, dealing with the complaining patient is of utmost priority. Here are some steps you and your staff may take to handle a complaining patient.

➢ Acknowledge the problem that happened. If something occurred in the process that is a problem for the patient, acknowledge it.

➢ Empathize with them. Try to understand their point of view. If we craft our servicescape with their experiences in mind, then we should have a good idea of how we want them to feel at a particular point in the process. If they don't feel that way, we have a starting point to address the complaint.

➢ Apologize for the problem. This might be enough for them. Saying, "I'm sorry this happened to you," might be enough for this patient. Don't stop there. If the problem continues to persist in the process, fix it.

➢ Own the problem. This step might be concerning for some people, especially risk management. However, if the problem occurred as a result of the process, owning simply means you will do what you can to fix the problem.

➢ Involve leadership when a problem/complaint is serious. If you're not at the top of the ladder, get your superiors involved in the problem. If you are the top, roll up your sleeves and get to work fixing the problem. Serious problems required serious work.

Most Customers Don't Complain

Don't rely on patient complaints to identify poor aspects of your service. If you are, then you will miss about half of the problems. A recent study showed 49% of dissatisfied customers don't complain in a restaurant. When in a store, 44% of dissatisfied customers don't complain. Half of all customers don't complain because they don't think it fixes anything. But believe me, they will complain. They will complain to their family, their friends, and all over the world wide web. They just won't complain to you. Encourage them to use comment cards, a feedback portal on your website, or another easy-to-use method of providing you feedback.

Develop a Culture of Service Quality

The quality of the service you offer is dependent upon the four Ps—the people, productivity or processes, performance or quality, and profitability. Creating the proper processes will help craft the culture that we want to deliver exemplary patient care, but it's our people, the folks who do the work, that is the key to quality care.

➢ **Hire the right people**. As I said earlier in the book, your people are the greatest asset you have. Take time to pick the right ones to fit your needs and your culture. Don't just hire the first person you meet. Resist the temptation to fill a position quickly. It's more of a headache to make a bad hire compared to dealing with not hiring anyone.

➤ **Educate and train them well**. Once you've hired the right people, invest in your assets. Provide training and education to them so they can perform at their highest level.

➤ **Empower them to fix anything**. Push all decision-making as low as you can in the organization. Most decisions can be made at the local level. For those decisions that you want to be a part of, make yourself available to deal with the questions, be patient with them, and provide prompt feedback. Don't leave them wondering what will happen next.

➤ **Recognize and reward them regularly**. Money doesn't motivate people if you're paying them a fair market rate. What motivates people is being recognized for the work they do. It's easy to criticize when we see something wrong. It's almost second nature. What seems difficult to do is give praise for work well done. Some would argue, "It's their job to work well." I would agree that you hired them to do a good job. However, it doesn't hurt to provide praise and recognize a job well done. If you aren't giving praise regularly, I challenge you to give genuine praise for a month purposefully. Keep a record of the changes you see in your people. You will be surprised at what happens.

➤ **Tell them everything, every day**. Be open with your people. Share important information with them early and often, even the bad news. You might be surprised, but someone might just have the answer you're looking for.

Takeaways

➤ How do you view your patients? Are they dependent upon you or are you dependent upon them? The answer to that question will change your perspective and how you treat patients.

> ➤ Just because no one is complaining doesn't mean all things are wonderful.
> ➤ There are many reasons why people complain. Identifying their reason for the complaint will help you determine the best of appropriate action to take.

17 | Benchmarking

Picking the right benchmark is incredibly vital to the success of your improvement plan. Pick the wrong ones, and you'll go astray and risk missing your targets.

What Is Benchmarking?

We hear all the time about benchmarks. What exactly is a benchmark? It's a measure or target of a process compared to a similar aspect of something else to learn and to improve performance. I got that from a process improvement textbook (which is why I wrote this book). Said in plain English, a benchmark is a standard by which we compare ourselves to measure our progress and quality. In service, benchmarking can become very challenging because we all don't begin with the same patient populations. Some of us take care of very sick patients. If we compare ourselves to a practitioner who only takes care of young, healthy people, our performance might look poor when, in fact, it's very good considering our patient population.

Why Do We Benchmark?

Benchmarking serves many purposes. First, it allows us to assess how well we're doing compared to other competing clinics. We all compete in a market, and benchmarking will enable us to see how we stack up against the competition.

It also helps us set realistic targets for our processes. If someone else gets results similar to what we want, then we know there is a way. We just have to figure it out. If no one is meeting a benchmark, then either the benchmark is too high, wrong, or just plain nuts.

Looking at someone's benchmarks can help us discover new ideas and ways to practice. It can prime our creative pumps and make the service we offer better.

Types of Benchmarks

There are three general types of benchmarking. Metric benchmarking helps us determine if what we're doing is relatively good or bad, but doesn't help us understand how we might be better. With practice benchmarking, we compare metrics, and we attempt to find new ideas and practices. We want to stimulate and improve our performance. Finally, process benchmarking is where we compare our process to that of another firm. However, those processes don't need to be within our market or even industry. We can often gain insight from other industries, much like healthcare, and anesthesiology has learned things from aviation safety. So we can examine and benchmark the process from other industries as well.

How to Benchmark

Picking a benchmark is part of the process; it's a metric we use to gauge our success. It's a piece of the puzzle. When we are selecting our benchmarks, we need to plan, then analyze, then adapt, and finally review the benchmark.

When we are planning to choose our benchmark, we should define the objectives of the metric. After that, we should determine the rate of change we desire, the rate of change that can be expected, and the rate of change we hope for.

Then we analyze the metric by comparing the practices and processes. Ask, "What do they do?" and "How do they do it?" What can we learn from the benchmark?

Armed with this data, we may adapt the information to our processes. We don't need to adopt their practices or processes, but we should adopt what we learn to redesign and implement the new information.

Finally, we need to review how things are going. How are we comparing to the benchmark? Are we gaining or losing ground? What's the progress we are making?

Use a Scorecard

If you don't keep track of what you are doing, how will you know if you are doing it well? Said another way, why do we track and trend vitals? Because we want to make sure we are effecting change and to identify when a bad trend is beginning. To help you track your metrics and benchmarks, create a scorecard to use as a quick visual reference aid.

First, identify key metrics and track them with a stoplight model. Use a Red/Yellow/Green coloring system to help you quickly identify those parameters that are in and out of control. Whether it is a leading or lagging metric, you will be able to target where you have process opportunity. For example, Red – the process needs some help; Yellow – the process needs to be watched; Green –the process is on target. Process owners should have a scorecard that they create, manage, and monitor. As the saying goes, you can't fix what you don't know.

Takeaways

> ➤ Benchmarks will help you determine how you compare to the competitors in the marketplace.
> ➤ When selecting your benchmarks, pick ones that reflect your patient population, size, resources, and agility.
> ➤ Don't stop with the numbers, but ask "What are they doing that allows them to perform at that level? How do they do it? Are we capable of achieving those benchmarks?

18 | My Checklist for Process Improvement

In this chapter, I'm going to walk you through the checklist I use to improve a process. I use this checklist in my personal life, professional business, and with clients. I use the simple four-step method of Plan-Do-Check-Act. Each section, **Plan, Do, Check**, and **Act** has it's own checklist that is to be used to ensure you don't miss important items during that phase of the process improvement plan.

Plan

Planning is the most critical part of any improvement initiative. This is my personal approach and checklist.

1. **Overall mission and purpose**. We begin here because it helps us stay focused on the reason the process exists.
   a. What is the service I provide to my patients? We should know what we are doing for the patient as a whole. Each process might offer something different, but they all should support the whole service.
   b. Why do I provide this service? What is the benefit to the patient? Understanding why we do what we do will help you stayed focused. Always ask, "Why is this step here? What is the benefit to the patient?"
   c. What problems are solved for the patient through my service?

    d. Do not skip this step. If you do, you risk scope creep and biting off more than you can chew.

2. **Define the current situation**. We must define our starting point if we are to improve. We will use the tools from earlier chapters to help us determine the current state of our system of processes.

    a. What's the current situation? What are the complaints? Where are the bottlenecks?

    b. Make observations.

    c. Conduct interviews with patients and appropriate staff.

    d. Identify the key people you should involve in the process improvement plan.

    e. Create a visual representation of the process. Make a map.

3. **The problems**. Problems are defined as those issues that prevent us from attaining our mission and purpose for the patient.

    a. What are the problems we have identified?

    b. Classify the problems. Some problems are broad and vague. Some are specific and easily defined. Then there are those problems that are low priority and have a low yield.

    c. **Identify the baggage**. What assumptions are we holding on to that will impair our improvement? What biases might be clouding our judgment?

4. **What we want**. Set targets. Once we have identified the map and defined the problems, we next set the course for the destination. We always set SMART targets. These are what we desire to occur. They are the end-results of our process.

    a. **Specific**. Make your targets as specific as possible. It'll be easier for you to track your progress if you do this.

    b. **Measurable**. Every goal should be measurable. Pick the metrics that provide meaningful and actionable data.

    c. **Achievable**. Our targets must be achievable. They should stretch us, but not to the point of frustration where we give up.

    d. **Realistic**. Considering your people, resources, and processes, set a realistic target.

    e. **Time-bound**. Set deadlines for your improvement targets. If we don't set deadlines, nothing ever gets done.

5. **Determine the root cause.**

    a. What should have happened?

    b. Why didn't it happen?

    c. Who could have prevented the problem?

    d. What could have prevented the problem?

Do

Now that we have completed the planning stage by setting targets, we must chart a course to achieve them.

1. **Gather ideas**. With your team in place, brainstorm ideas. Write the ideas down on a whiteboard, Post-It notes, or a big blank sheet of paper. After a while, you will begin to see patterns or similarities in the ideas. Group them together and begin making lists.

2. **Narrow the field**. Have your team begin to whittle down the list of prospective improvement actions. Pick the top ones to test or gather more information about.

3. **Revisit your top picks**. Reexamine each idea and ask the following questions to check its validity.

    a. Does it support the mission and purpose?

    b. Does it eliminate any complexity or confusion we identified in the planning phase?

    c. Will it meet our targets? Can we use it to achieve our SMART targets?

    d. Does it address the root cause of the problem?

    e. Does it pass a common-sense logical check?

4. **Implement the Action.** After we have determined the action we want to take, we take action

    a. **Generate buy-in**. Getting buy-in in a culture that supports and believes in the mission and purpose of the organization is easier. Remember, your culture begins with you and is carried out by those you hire. Still, change is hard for people, so you will have to get their confidence and commitment to change.

b. **Communicate!** Always be communicating. Communication is the leader's greatest tool. Get good at communication. Tell them why the change is happening, what the change will be, who will make the change, when it will occur, and how it will affect patient care. In your communication, illustrate how the change supports the mission and purpose. Discuss the root cause of the problem and the planned fix. Outline the timelines, metrics, and reporting processes. Discuss the financial impact of the problem and how long it will take to fix it. Supply the map of the process and distribute them with the people involved. Set the expectations of your people. If it's going to be rough, don't sugarcoat it. Be honest.

c. **Execute the plan**. Don't focus on perfection right out of the gate. Focus instead on changing the process and wait to see the desired change in behaviors. Be willing to adjust course when needed. However, adjust as little as possible during the trial period.

Check

After we begin the implementation phase of the change, we need to monitor our progress. We've already chosen the metrics and have begun collecting the data. Now we need to analyze it.

1. **Analyze our metrics**. Are our targets being achieved? What adjustments were necessary? Why? How are our people taking the change? What adjustments should we make?
2. **Document the results**. Revisit each action and verify it supported the mission and purpose. Ask if the patient experience changed the way we desired. Did we eliminate complexity? Was confusion reduced? Was the target met? Did we address the root cause of the problem? What is

the financial impact of the action? Are we better now than we were before? Share the answers to these questions with your team.

Act

With the change proven to be a success, it's now time to make it permanent.

1. **Standardize the process**. Are there any adjustments we need to make before implementing it on a larger scale?
2. **Define the roles and responsibilities**. Finalize who is responsible for what and clearly define the changes to the roles of those involved in the new process.
3. **Roll it out**. Create a document for the new process. Share it with everyone, even those not directly involved in the process. Doing so will help those either before or after the process to understand what happens.
4. **Review your progress at 3, 6, and 12 months**. Are your metrics still holding true? Is the change permanent? What new problems have occurred? Are they a result of the change? Change is constant, and you should constantly be working at change.

Conclusion

Well, that's it. That's how you improve any process. I hope you've learned a few things that you can immediately implement in your practice. As always, feel free to reach out to me for assistance. You can also learn about my online courses on this and other practice-related topics at www.davidnorrismdmba.com. I'm here to help you have the practice you desire.

Addendum

Plan-Do-Check-Act

Plan

Clarify the problem

> Begin with reviewing your overall mission and purpose.
> What service do you provide to your patients?
> Why do you provide this service?
> What problems are solved through your service?

Define the current situation

> What's the current situation?
> Observations
> Interviews
> Identify key people involved
> Create a visual of the process

Problem

> Problems
> Broad/vague issues
> Defined issues
> Low-priority issues

Set a target

> S - Specific
> M - Measurable
> A - Achievable
> R - Realistic
> T - Time-bound
> Set 1 to 5 goals this exercise should be able to achieve

Root cause

> What should have happened?
> Why did it not happen?
> Who could have prevented the problem?
> How could the problem have been prevented?
> Ask why at least five times

Do

Gather Ideas

> With your team, brainstorm ideas
> Post-It notes—group ideas and make lists
> Narrow down your choices to the top ones to test or further research

Revisit

> Reexamine each idea and test it with the following questions:
> Does it support the mission and purpose?
> Does it eliminate complexity or confusion identified in the planning phase?
> Will it meet your target and support your SMART goals and objectives?
> Does it address the root cause?
> Does it pass a common-sense logic check?

Define the Countermeasure

Document:
The countermeasure
Who is responsible
Who supports the responsible party
The steps needed to implement the countermeasure
The metrics you will use to gauge progress
The anticipated completion date (deadline)

Implement the Countermeasure

Generate buy-in
Communicate!
How does the problem relate to the mission and purpose?
The financial impact of the problem
The root cause of the problem
The determined countermeasure
Timelines, metrics, and reporting processes
Implement the countermeasure
Build and brief the implementation team
Stakeholder briefing items
Roles and responsibilities assigned publicly
Reporting methods
Change management
Build consensus during implementation
Manage expectations
Answer questions
Implement the countermeasure
Execute your plan
Don't focus on perfection
Focus on changing the process and the resultant change in behaviors
Be willing and able to adjust course when needed
Adjust as little as possible during the trial

Check

What's Your Progress?

Analyze your metrics at each milestone.
Are goals being achieved?
Are any adjustments needed?
Are there any morale or attitude issues?
Should any adjustments be made?

Document the Results

Revisit each countermeasure.
Did the change support the mission and purpose?
Was the patient experience improved?
Was complexity eliminated?
Was confusion eliminated?
Was target met, and did it support the objectives?
Revisit each countermeasure.
Was the root cause addressed?
Did positive change occur?
What was the financial impact of the countermeasure?
Are you better off now than before?

Act

Standardize the Process

Are any adjustments needed to implement on a larger scale?
Define the roles and responsibilities on a larger rollout.
Define timelines and milestones.

Roll It Out

Create document of new process.
Distribute new process diagram to everyone.

Create a step-by-step guide to help new users.
Document the lessons you've learned.
Review your progress at 6 months, then at 12 months.
Track metrics on a monthly basis.

About the Author

David J Norris, MD, MBA is a practicing cardiac anesthesiologist in Wichita, KS. He graduated from the University of Kansas School of Medicine and completed his residency in anesthesiology and fellowship in cardiac anesthesiology at Vanderbilt University Medical Center.

After receiving financial reports for his group, he realized he lacked the fundamental knowledge required to use these reports. This prompted him to obtain a Masters of Business Administration from Wichita State University. He now travels across the country teaching the fundamentals of business to others in healthcare. Dr. Norris speaks at a variety of conferences and works with clients to help them improve their business knowledge. His happiest moments are when fellow physicians call to discuss what they've learned from his books, articles, and talks.

Dr. Norris is still clinically active. He is happily married and has two children.

His first book, The Financially Intelligent Physician: What They Didn't Teach You in Medical School, is an excellent resource to help you determine the financial health of your practice and make solid business decisions. These two books will empower you to have the practice you desire.